RISK TAKING

RISK TAKING

A Managerial Perspective

Zur Shapira

RUSSELL SAGE FOUNDATION / NEW YORK

The Russell Sage Foundation

The Russell Sage Foundation, one of the oldest of America's general purpose foundations, was established in 1907 by Mrs. Margaret Olivia Sage for "the improvement of social and living conditions in the United States." The Foundation seeks to fulfill this mandate by fostering the development and dissemination of knowledge about the country's political, social, and economic problems. While the Foundation endeavors to assure the accuracy and objectivity of each book it publishes, the conclusions and interpretations in Russell Sage Foundation publications are those of the authors and not of the Foundation, its Trustees, or its staff. Publication by Russell Sage, therefore, does not imply Foundation endorsement.

Library of Congress Cataloging-in-Publication Data

Shapira, Zur.
   Risk taking : a managerial perspective / by Zur Shapira.
     p.   cm.
   Includes bibliographical references and index.
   ISBN 0-87154-766-X (hardbound)   ISBN 0-87154-767-8 (paperback)
   1. Risk management. 2. Decision-making. 3. Risk-taking
(Psychology). I. Title
HD61.S44 1994   94-21877
658.4'03—dc20   CIP

Text design: John Johnston.

RUSSELL SAGE FOUNDATION
112 East 64th Street, New York, New York 10021

10 9 8 7 6 5 4 3 2 1

To the memory of my mother

CONTENTS

LIST OF TABLES, FIGURES, AND APPENDIXES

Tables

Figures

Appendixes

PREFACE
AND ACKNOWLEDGMENTS

Risk taking is a major aspect of managerial work. It is also a characteristic of many choices, such as those involved with financial investment decisions. The pervasiveness of financial analysis in many work-related decisions, as well as in personal financial planning, has led to the proliferation of financial terminology. Thus, concepts like mergers and acquisitions and LBOs and junk bonds became household terms primarily in the 1980s. Almost all investors, irrespective of their level of sophistication, would be able to distinguish between stocks and bonds and would most likely say that the former are riskier but may provide higher returns.

The riskiness of a financial security is often captured by its volatility and is defined in classical decision models by the variance of the outcome distribution. Popular financial indicators, such as the Dow Jones Index or the Standard & Poor's 500, go up and down in patterns that cannot be predicted. The changes in these indexes (or in the price of a certain security) create a distribution which implies risk. In recent years, several anomalies in analyses of financial markets raised some questions as to whether a measure of a distribution (such as variance) truly captures the notion of risk.

In addition to its prominence in the financial world, risk exists in other domains. We witness daily risks and hazards in the environment, in technology, and in the medical industry. The concepts of risk in these domains fit more closely the dictionary definition of risk, which relates to danger, hazard, and the like. Although these terms have a predominantly negative connotation, risky choice entails positive aspects as well. After all, one makes a risky choice in hopes of getting a high return. It is these two aspects, the positive and the negative, which make risky choice play a central role in the analysis of decision under uncertainty.

Over the last 15 years, I have been teaching managers and MBA students in universities and in a variety of executive development programs. In teaching decision making, I would usually start by presenting the expected utility paradigm as a way of approaching risky choice. Once presented, I would ask whether the framework appeared meaningful and useful. In one of these programs an executive raised his hand and said that although the framework was interesting, "in real life you make decisions in a different way." When I probed him about his statement, he responded by saying that "in real life you weigh the options and then take a calculated risk." I asked if what I had just taught did not appear to him as a way of calculating risks. "Not entirely," said the executive, and proceeded to argue that in real choices you have to weigh the factors involved in the decision and then take a calculated risk. Apparently "calculated risk" in his terms meant something a little different from the calculation of expected utility.

Was that response merely an indication of semantic differences between academic language and real-life terminology? Perhaps partly so, but it may have reflected a deeper uneasiness with the usefulness of this analytical framework. Indeed, on several other occasions executives expressed their reservations about the method of expected utility and claimed that it was not helpful in making actual decisions.

I was intrigued by the manager's comments about the usefulness of the method for real-life decision making and decided to embark on an empirical study, interviewing managers in the field about the ways in which they actually approach risky choices. I interviewed a sample of fifty senior executives in the first stage of the study. Encouraged by the results of these interviews (see March and Shapira, 1987; Shapira, 1986), I decided to collect more data in the form of interviews as well as structured questionnaires. Eventually, I collected data from more than 700 managers, and the findings from this large study are reported in this book.

The scope of this study is very wide, and I would not have been able to complete it without the help of many people. My plan of studying managerial risk taking in the field matched the interest of the Russell Sage Foundation, where Marshall Robinson arranged for a grant that allowed me to carry the first stage of the study. A grant from the Recanati Foundation provided further support for starting the second stage of the research. I was later invited by Eric Wanner to spend a year at the Russell Sage Foundation as a Visiting Scholar, and it was during that year that I was able to complete the analyses of the data. While I was at the foundation, discussions with Eric Wanner, Peter de Janosi, Priscilla Lewis, and Lisa Nachtigall led me to the task of presenting the findings of the study in a monograph.

I was fortunate during the several stages of the study to be assisted by very able students: Gad Alon, Vered Dagan, Alan Eisner, Naomi Fink, Yael Ilan, Jeff Randolph, Yoni Roth, Grace Sone, Joe Tetzlaff, Bhatt Vadlamani, and Brian Wargon. Alaine Robertson has done a formidable job in typing the manuscript. During the years of my involvement with this project, I have benefited from discussions with several colleagues, including Menachem Brenner, Baruch Fischhoff, Rami Friedman, Dan Galai, Raghu Garud, Raanan Lipshitz, Praveen Nayyar, Agi Oldfield, Oscar Ornati, Guje Sevon, and Itzhak Venezia. Naturally, this project would have been difficult to complete without the continued support of my wife and two children. And finally, I owe a great debt to Jim March. His advice and encouragement have made this project a doable one.

Part 1

RISK IN MANAGERIAL DECISION MAKING

Chapter 1

THE ROLE OF RISK IN DECISION MAKING

INTRODUCTION

The increasing frequency with which the term *risk* appears in both the scientific and the popular publications is an indication of its importance in the public eye. In 1993 alone there were over 100 articles in the *New York Times* whose title included the word *risk*. For instance, a recent article entitled "Hidden Rules Often Distort Ideas of Risk" (Goleman, 1994) reviewed research by psychologists on the ranking of different activities and technologies in terms of their riskiness, including sports activities, food ingredients, and X rays and nuclear power. It appears that the public is preoccupied with the gauging of the risks involved in many aspects of modern life.

What is risk? The *Oxford English Dictionary* tells us that risk is "Hazard, chance of, or of bad consequences, loss." Two elements emerge from this definition, both having to do with the nature of the consequences of actions and the likelihood of such consequences. The emphasis is on negative consequences such as loss. The dictionary definition may fit the notion scientists have when they talk about risk, but it is too narrow when also looking at risk taking. Several studies have attempted to deal with this problem. Yates and Stone (1992) looked at the elements that can be the building blocks of the risk construct. Psychologists examined the personality correlates of risk (Kogan and Wallach, 1964) and the determinants of risk perception (Slovic, 1987). Researchers in economics (Knight, 1921), anthropology (Douglas and

Wildavsky, 1982), management (MacCrimmon and Wehrung, 1986; Sitkin and Pablo, 1992), and sociology (Heimer, 1988) have examined the role of risk in their respective fields of analysis. Risk and risk taking can be viewed from a multidisciplinary perspective. In that spirit, this book documents the results of a large-scale study of managerial perspectives on risk taking. To start, let us consider the definition of risk and its relation to action, as formulated in the field of decision making.

The classic treatment of risk in decision theory (Luce and Raiffa, 1957) distinguishes among three types of decision-making situations:

(a) *Certainty*, where each action is known to lead invariably to a particular outcome.

(b) *Risk*, where each action leads to a few known outcomes, each of which occurs with a specific probability.

(c) *Uncertainty*, where each action may lead to a set of consequences, yet the probabilities of these outcomes are unknown.

To illustrate these three situations, consider the investment in treasury bills, which is often defined as a "sure" or "riskless" asset. If a person holds treasury bills until maturity, she can calculate with certainty the exact amount of interest she will receive. This scenario can therefore represent the situation of *certainty*. A situation of *risk* is often described by the analogue of flipping a fair coin. A person knows what the outcomes are, as well as their probabilities, though she cannot be certain which outcome (heads or tails) will occur. Finally, *uncertainty* can be exemplified by buying a particular stock on the New York Stock Exchange. Someone knows that the price of the stock on the following day may be higher, the same, or lower than the purchase price. However, she has no way of knowing the exact probability of any of these outcomes.

It can be argued that there is a major difference between certainty, on the one hand, and the two other situations, on the other. A risky situation is, therefore, one in which the decision maker is not sure which outcome will occur. This uncertainty may lead to an erroneous choice and, eventually, a loss. What would be a reasonable choice criterion in such a situation? The literature on risky choice can be classified as being part of the *normative* or the *descriptive* approach. The normative approach suggests some rules for choice under risk. The term *normative* implies that the suggested rule is the best under certain conditions and, thus, tells people how they *should* make choices under risk. The descriptive approach takes a different route; instead of telling decision makers how they should make choices, it looks at the ways people actually make decisions in situations involving risk and tries to come up with models that describe what they do. As we will see later, people often do not behave according to the rules recommended by normative models.

NORMATIVE APPROACHES TO RISKY CHOICE

There are two main normative rules for choice under risk: the expected value rule and the expected utility rule.

The Expected Value Rule

Statistical decision theory suggests that *expected value* is the best rule for choice under risk (Raiffa, 1968). A simple game situation will illustrate this criterion. Suppose someone is playing a game of tossing a fair coin. He is to guess what side the coin will fall on. If he guesses correctly, he will win $10, but if he is wrong, he will win nothing. How much is he willing to pay for participating in this game? In other words, how much is such a game worth to him? There is no single, correct answer to this question. Some values people provide in responding are $10, $5, and $0. Of those, the one in the middle ($5) fits the statistical decision theory approach. The choice of $5 can be analyzed as follows: There are only two possible outcomes of the coin toss, heads or tails. Furthermore, because the coin is fair, the chance for each of the outcomes is one-half. Thus, the two outcomes, $10 and $0, are equally likely, and their average would seem to be the appropriate price of the game. The notion of expected value is precisely that: Multiply the outcomes by their respective probabilities and sum them up. Hence, the expected value of this game is $5 ($1/2 \times \$10 + 1/2 \times \$0 = \$5$). This is the way to calculate weighted averages, except that, in calculating expected values, outcomes are multiplied by probabilities rather than by relative frequencies.

Would someone be willing to pay up to $5.00 to participate in this game? Many would; indeed, often when this example is presented in classes on decision making, managers come up with monetary values close to $5.00 (say $4.90, leaving some room for profit) in accordance with the expected value rule.

Consider a slightly different game that involves repeated flips of a fair coin. There is a simple rule that governs the game: The person must guess the outcome of the coin flip, and the first time she succeeds in guessing, the game is over. For instance, if she guesses tails on the first flip and is wrong, then guesses tails again for the second flip and is right, the game is over after the second flip. To lure a person into playing the game, monetary rewards are offered. The reward schedule is as follows: If the person correctly guesses the first flip, she wins $2 and the game is over. If she is wrong in the first guess but correct in the second, she wins $4 and the game is over. In general, if she is wrong $(n - 1)$ times but correct on the nth trial, she wins 2^n and the game is over. It turns out that this may be quite a hefty reward; for instance, if she is wrong nine times but correct on the tenth trial, she earns $1,024 $(= \$2^{10})$. Obviously, the optimal strategy would be to make as many wrong guesses as possible until the one correct guess that terminates the game.

The question is how much a person would be willing to pay to participate in this game. When making the decision, it must be kept in mind that this game is played once; it is over when one correct guess is made. This may happen on the first, the second, or any later trial. Surprisingly, people do not want to bet much on this game. Often when I present this game in a decision-making class, many do not offer to pay more than $2.50 to participate in the game. How would one go about calculating the price for this game?

The method of expected value proposes a way. To calculate expected value, one needs to consider the probabilities and pay-offs for games ending at different trials. For example, the probability of the game's ending on the first trial is one-half. Furthermore, since each flip of the coin at any trial is independent of prior trials, the probability of guessing wrong (or correctly) at each trial is one-half. Therefore, the probability of the game's terminating on the second trial is $1/2 \times 1/2 = 1/4$. Consequently, the probability that the game would be over on the third trial is $1/2 \times 1/2 \times 1/2 = 1/8$. In general, the probability that the game will terminate on the nth trial is $(1/2)^n$. Using the expected value rule, one needs to multiply the probabilities by the respective payoffs for every trial and add these products up. To facilitate this calculation, the respective probabilities, payoffs, and their products are presented in Table 1.1. As can be seen, the product for each trial equals 1. When all the outcomes are added up, and because the game can theoretically never end, we get the sum of an infinite number of 1s, or infinity.

It may be puzzling that people are willing to pay only $2.50 to participate in this game. Indeed, similar responses puzzled Daniel Bernoulli, who offered the previous gamble to fellow mathematicians and published the results in 1738 in a study that became known as the St. Petersburg Paradox. Trying to account for the apparent departure from the use of expected value, Bernoulli (1738) postulated that, when approaching risky choices, people

Table 1.1 A flip-of-the-coin-game.

Game: Your task is to correctly guess the outcome of a flip of a coin. The game lasts until one makes a correct guess (then it can start again). The reward structure is as follows:

Game Ends on Trial No.	Payoff	Probability of Winning	Payoff x Probability
1	$2	1/2	$1
2	$4	1/4	$1
3	$8	1/8	$1
.	.	.	.
.	.	.	.
.	.	.	.
.	.	.	.
.	.	.	.
10	$1024	1/1024	$1
n	$2^n	$1/2^n$	$1
.	.	.	.
.	.	.	.

Note: Expected Value = 1 + 1 + 1 + ... + 1 + + + ... = (infinity)

do not simply use the face value of the outcomes (such as monetary values). Rather, they use some psychological value of these outcomes, which he termed the *utility of outcomes*. According to Bernoulli, a reasonable utility function that described the choices of his respondents was a concave function such as the one described in Figure 1.1. Examples of the type of function displayed in Figure 1.1 are the logarithmic function and the square root function. Applying the latter to the analysis of the problem reveals that a person who has such a utility function should be willing to pay only $2.93 for the game, although its expected value is infinity. The calculation of the expected utility for the square root function is provided in Appendix 1.

The Expected Utility Rule

The expected utility rule is a simple transformation of the expected value rule. It is still a summation of probabilities times their respective values, except that the values are subjective values called *utilities*, rather than the actual monetary values.

The utility function of a person serves as a measure of that person's risk tendencies. In general, a linear function describes a *risk-neutral* person; a concave function, a *risk-averse* person; and a convex function, a *risk-seeking* person. These terms are defined as follows. Consider the flip of a fair coin where, if a person correctly guesses the outcome, he gets $10 and, if he guesses

Figure 1.1   A concave utility function.

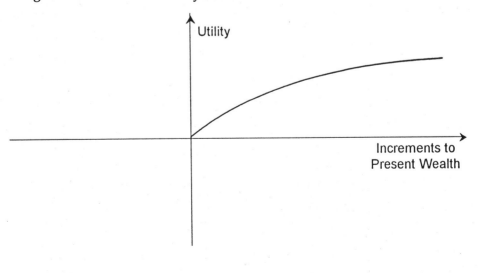

incorrectly, he gets nothing. The two outcomes are of equal probability, and the expected value of the gamble is $5. The expected value is also considered to be the value of the gamble if a person were to bet on it. Suppose that someone is offered the choice of playing this game or receiving a sure $5 without gambling. If the person is indifferent between the gamble (whose expected value is $5) or the $5 payment, he is defined as *risk neutral.* Many people, however, prefer receiving a sure $5 to taking part in such a gamble. People who prefer a certain cash equivalent over a gamble with a similar expected value are called *risk averse.* Conversely, these who prefer a gamble with a certain expected value over a sure payment that is equal to the expected value are called *risk seeking.* The expected utility principle has been proposed as the optimal criterion for choice under uncertainty, because it takes into account individual risk tendencies (Von Neumann and Morgenstern, 1944). Does this rule of choice do a good job of describing people's choices among risky prospects? Consider the following example.

Suppose that a person is required to play one of the two gambles in each of the two situations shown below (see Allais, 1953):

Situation I

Gamble A: 100% chance of winning $1/2 million

Gamble B: 10% chance of winning $2 1/2 million
              89% chance of winning $1/2 million
              1% chance of winning 0

Situation II

Gamble C: 11% chance of winning $1/2 million
              89% chance of winning 0

Gamble D: 10% chance of winning $2 1/2 million
              90% chance of winning 0

Which gamble would she choose in Situation I and which in Situation II? Most people choose Gamble A in Situation I and Gamble D in Situation II. Such a pattern of choice violates the expected utility rule. Preferring Gamble A over Gamble B implies that

$$U(\text{Gamble A}) > U(\text{Gamble B}),$$

where U indicates utility. It follows that $U(1/2) > .10\ U(2\ 1/2) +$ .89 $U(1/2) + .01\ U(O)$, where $(1/2)$ and $(2\ 1/2)$ designate $1/2 million and \$2 1/2 million, respectively. It can also be assumed, without loss of generality, that $U(0) = 0$ and, hence, this inequality can be written as

$$U(1/2) > .10\ U(2\ 1/2) + .89\ U(1/2)$$

$$\text{or } .11\ U(1/2) > .10\ U(2\ 1/2).$$

The preference for Gamble D over Gamble C in Situation II implies that, assuming $U(0) = 0$,

$$.10 U(2\ 1/2) > .11\ U(1/2),$$

which is inconsistent with the inequality derived from the preference in the first situation. This example suggests that, in choosing among options, people may not use the expected utility combination rule. Rather, it is likely that in choosing Gamble A over Gamble B, people exhibit a strong preference for the certainty of Gamble A. Hence, they may not calculate expected utilities but choose the certain option, thus making their choice on the probability dimension. In contrast, in choosing among two uncertain options with similar chances (Gamble D over Gamble C), people presumably go by the payoff and do not consider the probability dimension. Indeed, the difference between probabilities of .11 and .10 is perceived as negligible and may not be taken into account.

It should be noted that, in many decision-making situations, precise objective probabilities are not available. For instance, there is no objective probability for the price of securities traded on, say, the New York Stock Exchange on an upcoming trading day. If someone wishes to use the expected utility principle, probabilities have to be estimated. Such estimates can be only subjective. Savage (1954) suggested the principle of *subjective expected utility* to account for the application of expected utility with subjective probabilities. Since most risky choices refer to future states of the world, the notion of subjective probabilities is fundamental to models of risky choice.

Some Empirical Evidence

The possibility that people apply simplified decision-making rules such as choosing either by comparing the monetary amounts (without taking the probability element into account) or according to the probability dimension by preferring alternatives with certainty over uncertain ones (without taking into calculation the amounts) may be typical of situations such as those described in Allais's (1953) paradox. Real-life events that partially mimic these situations are the purchase of insurance and of lottery tickets. These situations are characterized as high consequence–low probability events. Economists have long been puzzled by the fact that the same person may buy both insurance and lottery tickets, the former being a display of risk aversion and the latter, of risk seeking. In an attempt to account for such behavior Friedman and Savage (1948) proposed a special utility function with alternating segments that may account for the risk-seeking behavior of purchasing lottery tickets. Engaging in the purchase of both insurance and lottery tickets is still considered an anomaly from the perspective of the theory of rational choice.

Empirical studies of the purchase of either insurance or lottery tickets failed to provide support for the use of expected utility in real choices. In a survey of over 3,000 homeowners who lived in either flood-prone or earthquake-prone areas in the United States, Kunreuther et al. (1978) found that the purchase of insurance policies in those populations differed dramatically from what would be predicted by the normative approach. In an analysis of the purchase of state lottery tickets, Shapira and Venezia (1992) found that the demand for lottery tickets was related to the size of the first prize but not to its expected value. These and other empirical tests suggest that the normative expectation rule may have limited power in describing actual risky-choice behavior. It appears that, in many risky-choice situations, people do not seem to behave in a way that is compatible with the maximization of expected utility.

DESCRIPTIVE APPROACHES TO RISKY CHOICE

In many decision-making situations the amount of data required for making a rational choice may be overwhelming. For instance, there are over 1,700 securities on the New York Stock Exchange, whose prices are changing continuously and simultaneously. Several principles were developed to help simplify such decision-making situations, prominent among them being Simon's (1955) *satisficing* principle. Other theories were developed to account for the human tendency to restructure decision alternatives with regard to a common reference point, culminating in a simple notion of gain versus loss of the alternative. The most well known of these is prospect theory (Kahneman and Tversky, 1979).

The Satisficing Principle

One of the roots of the field called *behavioral decision theory* has been Simon's (1947) seminal work on administrative decision making. Simon's (1955) behavioral model of rational choice further elaborated on the idea of satisficing. According to this model in simplifying choice problems, decision makers consider alternatives in only a subset of the entire set of alternatives. They then select the best alternative from this subset; thus, the process does not necessarily end with the optimal alternative being chosen. Rather, the satisficing principle suggests that people search through a limited set until they find a good enough alternative. As part of his model, Simon (1955) proposed a step type utility function corresponding to "win" and "lose" states. Such a function can approximate a continuous utility function under certain conditions.

Simon's (1955) work stimulated further research on organizational decision making (March and Simon, 1958) and on managerial behavior as a search process (Cyert and March, 1963). In particular, March (1988a) developed the idea that managerial behavior can be described by means of attention paid to conflicting goals. This work has been extended to the area of managerial risk taking (March and Shapira, 1987, 1992).

Prospect Theory

Kahneman and Tversky (1979) developed a model of choice under risk that accounts for paradoxes such as the one by Allais (1953) presented earlier. Consider the following experiment, which requires a person to choose one gamble in Situation I and one gamble in Situation II.

Situation I

    Gamble A: sure win of $400

    Gamble B: 50% chance of winning $1,000

                 50% chance of winning $0

Situation II

    Gamble C: sure loss of $400

    Gamble D: 50% chance of losing $1,000

                 50% chance of losing $0

Most people prefer Gamble A over Gamble B, and Gamble D over Gamble C. Situation I depicts risk aversion and Situation II, risk seeking. Kahneman and Tversky (1979) thus proposed prospect theory to account for this pattern of risky choice. Prospect theory has three elements to it: a value function that plays the role of a utility function in utility theory, a decision weights function that plays the role of probabilities in utility theory, and an editing rule. Uncertain prospects are characterized by the value function and the decision weights function. The values are multiplied by the respective decision weights and summed up in a similar manner to expected utility.

The value function is presented in Figure 1.2. It has three characteristics. First, it defines values as deviations from a certain reference point. Second, both gains and losses diminish in value, suggesting that people are more sensitive to changes around the reference point. Third, it is steeper for losses than for gains, reflecting the assumption that people are more sensitive to losing a certain amount than to gaining the same amount. A major aspect of the value function is the reference point. Although, in general, many points can play the role of a reference, Kahneman and Tversky (1979) proposed that the asset position also plays the role of adaption level (Helson, 1964), hence implying an almost instantaneous adjustment to a new asset position. Thus, wealth does not matter much, because if a person wins $1 million, she will immediately adapt to this new wealth and respond in a risk-averse manner to the gambles in Situation I and in a risk-seeking manner to the gambles in Situation II. Conceiving of the value function as describing the psychophysics of money, Kahneman and Tversky (1979) argued that changes in wealth are a more important determinant of risky choice than the absolute value of wealth. That is, within a very wide

Figure 1.2 Prospect theory type value function.

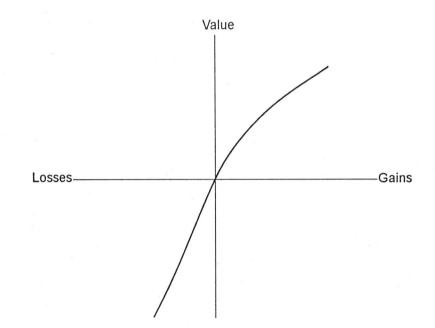

range of options, a millionaire and a poor person would respond in a similar way to the gambles in the situations just described.

An important feature of prospect theory is the editing rule. Given a choice between risky alternatives, decision makers "edit" the choice problem until they arrive at a simple choice between edited alternatives that can be compared in either the domain of gains or the domain of losses. The editing feature was later transformed to the concept of *framing* (Tversky and Kahneman, 1981), which has many implications for a wide range of decision-making situations. In particular, it was shown that many problems can be positioned in both a positive frame (thus leading to risk aversion) and a negative frame (thereby leading to risk seeking). These framing effects pose significant hurdles to normative theories of risky choice.

NORMATIVE AND DESCRIPTIVE PERSPECTIVES: A COMPARISON

The normative approach to risky choice emphasizes the statistical basis for decision making. When there are large samples of repeated events, expected values provide the most sound summary statistic for choice under risk. In the expected value formula, the most likely outcome gets the highest weight, and the least likely outcome gets the lowest weight. Furthermore, utility theory proposes that the subjective value of outcomes be calculated, and, following Savage's (1954) suggestion, subjective probabilities are entered instead of objective ones. The normative approach proposed by Von Neumann and Morgenstern (1944) essentially calls for the use of the expectation rule for choice under risk.

The descriptive approach to risky choice stemmed from studies showing that people did not use the expectation rule in making choices among risky prospects (Edwards, 1954). Simon's (1955) notion of satisficing is a search rule that was developed to describe how decision makers operated, given human limitations on information availability and information processing. Prospect theory pushed the descriptive approach even further by suggesting that people choose among risky prospects through a process in which they edit the alternatives and compare them using some reference point. Furthermore, decision weights are used in calculation rather than probabilities.

Beginning around 1970, evidence has been growing of the incompatibility of the two approaches. The normative approach tells people what they should do, whereas the descriptive approach is an attempt to get an account of what people actually do. Initially, decision analysts hoped that documenting biases from the normative model and then pointing them out to decision makers would solve the problem. Such a remedial approach did not succeed, and arguments were made for developing a descriptive model of choice behavior. Yet, as Bell, Raiffa, and Tversky (1988) noted, the evidence that had accumulated thus far suggested that only through developing normative, descriptive, and prescriptive models of choice could improvements in decision making be achieved.

These comments indicate that the differences among approaches are of major importance for studying risk taking. In particular, one may ask whether the differences between the normative approach to risk and the behavior of people who make risky choices are consistently demonstrated. Are those differences significant enough to warrant attention? This book attempts to deal with these issues. It reports the results of a study in which some 700 managers participated. The findings suggest that the answers to both of these questions are affirmative; that is, there are consistent and meaningful differences between the normative model and the risky choice behavior of managers, and these differences warrant our attention. The major findings are briefly discussed in the next section.

THE PRESENT STUDY: SOME DIFFERENCES FROM THE NORMATIVE APPROACH

The ways managers define risk and react to risks are quite different from normative decision theory. In particular, it appears that

(a) Managers are quite insensitive to estimates of probabilities of possible outcomes. This appears not to be a bias; rather, they feel much more at home with detailed descriptions of particular events, such as "the worst possible outcome," than with summary statistics. One factor that contributes to this insensitivity is the (often erroneous) belief that risk can be controlled. The concept of probability in itself has a connotation of events that are random and not controllable. Such notions are contradictory to the conceptions of executives about the essence of risk taking.

(b) Inherent in the calculation of expected value is the equal weighing of probabilities and outcome values. This notion was repeatedly rejected by managers. In most cases, outcome values appeared to have a more central role than probabilities. Furthermore, managers often described the way they evaluated risky options as attending to events at the extreme ends of the distribution. They commented that summarizing the information using a combination rule such as expected value may miss the most important ingredients of the picture.

(c) Managers worry much more about actual losses than they think about opportunity losses. The probability distribution of possible outcomes has positive outcomes as well as negative ones. The former play a minor role in managerial concepts of risk. For managers, risk is "downside risk," which is similar to the notion of danger, hazard, and so on. Calculation of expected values and variances, on the other hand, is not affected by whether an outcome is positive or negative.

ASPECTS OF A DESCRIPTIVE MODEL
OF MANAGERIAL RISK TAKING

These managers were familiar with using expected values and variances to analyze risky alternatives. The fact that they voiced dissatisfaction with the normative approach cannot be attributed to ignorance. Furthermore, it appears that simple corrective procedures, or incentives, are not going to eliminate the discrepancies between their behavior and the normative approach. Their behavior indicates a different mode of processing risk both cognitively and emotionally. Elements of this different mode include (1) focusing on a few discrete values (events) in the outcome distribution; (2) sequentially attending to critical performance targets, of which survival is the most salient; (3) dealing with risk in a dynamic process in which estimates are modified, parameters are changed, and the problem is restructured in an active manner.

In this dynamic-active process, the importance of careful probability estimates gets dimmed. Because many of the choices executives make are unique, nonrepeated types, the value of standard statistical analyses seems less important. Unfortunately, ignoring such analyses may lead to the development of unfounded beliefs about causal relations. Perhaps an attempt to model such processes should focus on the construction of scenarios in situations where probability distributions are nonstationary.

It can be argued that market forces will eliminate those who do not follow the normative model. Yet, there is growing evidence that, even in the relatively efficient financial markets, certain discrepancies prevail (Thaler, 1990). Furthermore, a large portion of managerial risk taking is done in situations that hardly resemble an efficient market. Therefore, the discrepancies between the normative and the behavioral models do warrant attention. The purpose of this book is not to provide evidence counter to decision theory but to draw implications for understanding decision making in organizations and for the engineering of risk taking and risk management.

BOOK PLAN

This book consists of three parts. The second chapter of the first part elaborates on the characteristics of risk and risk taking. In the second part of the book, the empirical study is described. Chapter 3 documents the methodology of the study. It details the procedure and describes the participants. It also discusses the advantages and disadvantages of alternative methods of studying risk taking. Chapter 4 analyzes managers' responses regarding the definition of risk. Chapter 5 describes and analyzes managers' attitudes toward risk. Chapter 6 provides an account of how managers deal with risk.

The third part of the book contains a discussion of a possible descriptive model of managerial risk taking. In Chapter 7 the cognitive aspects of risk taking are explored. In Chapter 8 the role of incentives and motivation in risk taking is discussed. The final chapter scrutinizes the organizational context, raises the issue of responsibility costs, and considers the prospects for improving managerial risk taking. Finally, an epilogue throws some light on the study in a retrospective manner.

Chapter 2

CHARACTERISTICS OF RISK
AND RISK TAKING

SOME ADDITIONAL ASPECTS OF RISK

In Chapter 1 the expected value criterion was introduced as a rule for risky choice. There are, of course, other criteria for choosing among risky alternatives, although the criterion of expected value has attributes that make it rather attractive. What does a person do if two alternatives have the same expected value? Consider the game where someone could choose between definitely receiving $5 or a flip of a coin that would get her $10 or nothing. Suppose that, in addition to the previous game, there is another game where the outcomes of the toss of a fair coin are $7 for a correct guess and $3 for a wrong guess. The expected value of the second game is also $5, but most people would define it as less risky than the first game. Therefore, on top of the uncertainty factor described in Chapter 1, an additional element has to be introduced to describe risky situations, which has to do with the variability, or variance, of the outcomes.

Volatility and Risk

A basic characteristic of risk is *volatility*. The Dow Jones Industrials Index, for example, goes up and down in a pattern that cannot be predicted. The changes in this index (or in the price of a certain security) create a distribution that implies risk. The *variance* of the distribution is a natural candidate for being a measure of risk. Indeed, it was a cornerstone in the *mean-variance* approach to the analysis of decision under uncertainty (Markowitz, 1959). This approach suggests that, in choosing among risky alternatives, people should consider both the expected value (or return) and the variance of the probability distribution over the possible outcomes. The criteria for choice suggest that, if two alternatives have the same variance, a person should choose the alternative with the highest expected value. If, on the other hand, the two alternatives have the same expected value, should a person choose the alternative with the smaller variance? Obviously, it depends on the person's risk tendencies. The idea that people should base their choices among gambles on the variances of the gambles, as well as on their expected values, was proposed a long time ago by Fisher (1906). Yet, as Coombs, Dawes, and Tversky (1970) argued, the question as to what criterion should be used to combine expectations and variances for a rule of risky choice is rather difficult to answer. Furthermore, there may be other dimensions that are important in choosing among risky prospects. For instance, if the distribution of outcomes is very wide, perhaps rules that put weight on its extreme values (such as maximin or maximax) would do a better job of explaining people's choices.

Ambiguity and Risk

Suppose that someone is required to participate in the following game. There are two bags, each containing 100 balls. In the first bag there are 50 blue balls and 50 red balls. In the second bag there are 100 blue and red balls in unknown proportion. The game is a single-step game. The person must draw one ball from the bag of his choice, guessing its color. If correct, the person gets a prize of $10, and if he is wrong, he gets nothing. Which bag does he draw the ball from? It turns out that most people prefer to draw a ball from the 50:50 bag, although it could be shown that such a choice violates the additivity assumption of utility theory. Ellsberg (1961), who ran this experiment, termed the finding *ambiguity effect*. Ellsberg claimed that people were averse to risky choices where probabilities were not specified, and he assumed that people would avoid choosing ambiguous alternatives.

Kunreuther, Hogarth, and Meszaros (1993) demonstrated ambiguity aversion with data collected on underwriters and actuaries from insurance companies. Ambiguity was defined as the case where two experts gave different estimates, though their mean estimate was the same as the estimate of the other alternative on which the experts concurred. Heath and Tversky (1991) have shown that ambiguity effects may be moderated by the confidence people have in their judgment and skills.

It appears that there may be quite a few dimensions that characterize risk. Terms such as *uncertainty*, *ignorance*, *incomplete knowledge*, and *ambiguity* all relate to risk and may highlight slightly different perspectives.

Risk Taking in Real Settings

The discussion in Chapter 1 focused on criteria for choice among risky alternatives. The individual making the choice is pictured by this process as a passive agent. He presumably has stable attitudes toward risk and, given distributional information, will choose the alternative that will maximize his expected utility (according to the normative approach) or simply choose the best among the alternatives considered (according to the satisficing rule). The previous discussion of volatility muddies the water a bit for the use of the expectation principle. Adding the problem of ambiguity makes the use of normative rules of choice even more problematic. There is, however, an additional complication for calculation-based models of risky choice. It stems from the fact that, when undertaken in a real setting, risky choice is a dynamic-active endeavor that often bears little resemblance to the ordered world of statistical decision theory. The evidence on risk taking by executives (MacCrimmon and Wehrung, 1986; Shapira, 1986) and other professionals (Keyes, 1985) suggests that a better understanding of risk and risk taking can be achieved by studying risk taking in realistic settings.

In realistic situations involving risky choices, three aspects are of major concern to decision making. First, how is risk defined in the particular situation? Second, what are the attitudes of the decision makers toward risk? Are they risk averse, neutral, or risk seeking? Third, what can be done to choose the best alternative or to manage the risk? These three aspects—definition of risk, attitudes toward risk, and dealing with risk—are needed for a complete description of the process of risk taking. Any decision model starts with a definition of the problem (hence the definition of risk), continues with the decision maker's tendencies and values (hence, attitudes toward risk), and ends with the phase of evaluation, choice, and postdecision behavior, which is handled here under the title of dealing with risk. The classical and behavioral approaches to risk are discussed and compared along these aspects.

CLASSICAL AND BEHAVIORAL APPROACHES TO RISK AND RISK TAKING[1]

Definition of Risk

In classical decision theory, risk is most commonly conceived of as reflecting variation in the distribution of possible outcomes, their likelihoods, and their subjective values. Risk is measured either by nonlinearities in the revealed utility of money or by the variance of the probability distribution of possible gains and losses associated with a particular alternative (Pratt, 1964; Arrow, 1965). In the latter formulation, a risky alternative is one for which the variance is large; and risk is one of the attributes that, along with the expected value of the alternative, are used in evaluating alternative gambles. The idea of risk is embedded, of course, in the larger idea of choice as affected by the expected return of an alternative. Theories of choice assume that decision makers prefer larger expected returns to smaller ones, provided all other factors (e.g., risk) are constant (Lindley, 1973). It is also assumed that decision makers prefer smaller risks to larger ones, provided other factors (e.g., expected value) are the same (Arrow, 1965). Thus, expected value is assumed to be positively associated, and risk is assumed to be negatively associated, with the attractiveness of a risky alternative.

Agreeing on an empirical definition of risk within this frame-

[1]This section draws on March and Shapira (1987).

work has proven difficult. Simple measures of mean and variance lead to empirical observations that can be interpreted as being off the mean-variance frontier. This has led to efforts to develop modified conceptions of risk, particularly in studies of financial markets. Early criticisms of variance definitions of risk (Markowitz, 1952) as confounding downside risk with upside opportunities led to a number of efforts to develop models based on semi-variance (Coombs, 1983; Fishburn, 1977; Porter, 1974). Both variance and semi-variance ideas of risk, however, have been shown not to agree with Von Neumann and Morgenstern's (1944) axioms except under rather narrow conditions (Levy and Markowitz, 1979; Levy and Sarnat, 1984); and this result has stimulated efforts to estimate risk and risk preference from observed securities prices. This procedure is essentially the approach of much of the contemporary literature on risk in finance. One example is the capital asset pricing model that had become one standard approach to financial analysis (Sharpe, 1964, 1977). It defines the degree to which a given portfolio co-varies with the market portfolio as the systematic risk. The residual (in a regression sense) is defined as nonsystematic, or specific, risk. These elaborations have contributed substantially to the understanding of financial markets, but the risk-return implications of the model have not always found empirical support (Gibbons, 1982; Fama, 1991).

There are many other complications with decision theoretic conceptions of risk when they are taken as descriptions of the actual processes underlying choice behavior. There are suggestions, for example, that individuals tend to ignore possible events that are very unlikely or very remote, regardless of their consequences (Kunreuther, et al., 1978). There are suggestions that individuals look at only a few possible outcomes, rather than at the whole distribution, and measure variation with respect to those few points (Boussard and Petit, 1967; Alderfer and Bierman, 1970). It has been posited that decision makers are more comfortable with verbal characterizations of risk than with numerical characterizations, even though the translation of verbal-risk expressions into numerical form shows high variability and context dependence (Budescu and Wallsten, 1985). There are suggestions that the probabilities of outcomes and their values enter into calculations of risk independently, rather than as their products (Slovic, Fischhoff, and Lichtenstein, 1977). Such ideas seem to indicate that the ways in which decision makers define risk may differ significantly from the definitions of risk in the theoretical literature and that different individuals see the same risk situation in quite different ways (Kahneman and Tversky, 1982; Yates, 1992).

In sum, there is growing evidence of a substantial disparity between the classical model and the actual way people define risk and its elements. New attempts by decision theorists and economists to develop new variants on the expected utility paradigm such as rank dependent utility models (e.g., Quiggin, 1982; Yaari, 1987, Weber, 1994) have proved successful in accounting for some departures from models of rational choice behavior, but not for others.

Attitudes Toward Risk

Classical analyses by Pratt (1964), Arrow (1965), and others, as well as more recent work (Ross, 1981), assumed that individual human decision makers are risk averse, that is, when faced with one alternative having a given outcome with certainty and with a second alternative that is a gamble but has the same expected value as the first, an individual will choose the certain outcome, rather than the gamble. Thus, it follows that decision makers would normally have to be compensated for variability in possible outcomes; and the greater the return on investment that is observed in a situation, the greater should be the variance involved. Levy and Sarnat (1984) studied twenty-five years of investments in mutual funds and discovered that investors were averse to the variance of returns. Nevertheless, the fact that people gamble, buy lottery tickets, or engage in both is strong evidence against the assumption about the pervasiveness of risk aversion.

Managers may not necessarily believe, however, that risk and return are positively correlated. Some studies of mergers (Brenner and Shapira, 1983; Mueller, 1969) suggest that this is not the case. Moreover, the aggregate data yield ambiguous results. Bowman (1980) has shown a negative relation between traditional risk (i.e., simple variance) and average return across industries using accounting data. This paradox has been explained in part by Fiegenbaum and Thomas (1986) using prospect theory, although the debate continues to rage. However, recent research in finance has also shown that there is no significant relationship between average return and systematic risk of common stocks (Fama and French, 1993).

Attitudes toward risk are often described as stable properties of individuals, perhaps related to aspects of personality development or culture (Douglas and Wildavsky, 1982); and efforts have been made to associate risk preference with dimensions of personality such as achievement motivation (McClelland, 1961; Deci, 1975; Kogan and Wallach, 1964) or locus of control (McInish, 1982). Global differences between presumed risk takers and others within a culture, profession, or job have, however, remained relatively elusive. For example, Brockhaus (1980) attempted to study the risk taking propensities of entrepreneurs. The individuals who quit their managerial jobs and became owners of business or managers of business ventures were compared to regular managers. Using the questionnaire on choice dilemmas of Kogan and Wallach, he found no differences in risk propensity among the different groups.

It is possible that risk preference is partly a stable feature of individual personality, but a number of variable factors such as mood (Hastorf and Isen, 1982), feelings (Johnson and Tversky, 1983), and the way in which problems are framed (Tversky and Kahneman, 1981) also appear to affect perception of and attitudes toward risk. In particular, Kahneman and Tversky (1979) have observed that, when dealing with a risky alternative whose possible outcomes are generally good (e.g., positive monetary outcomes), human subjects appear to be risk averse; but if they are dealing with a risky alternative whose possible outcomes are generally poor, human subjects tend to be risk seeking. This pattern of context dependence is familiar to students of risk taking by animals (Kamil and Roitblat, 1985), individuals (Griffith, 1949; Snyder, 1978; Laughhunn, Payne, and Crum, 1980; Payne, Laughhunn, and Crum, 1981), and organizations (Mayhew, 1979; Bowman, 1982). It forms the basis for several modern treatments of context-dependent risk taking (Maynard-Smith, 1978; Kahneman and Tversky, 1979; Lopes, 1987; March, 1988b; March and Shapira, 1992).

There are unresolved problems, however. The idea of risk taking in the face of adversity certainly finds support, but the idea that major innovations and change are produced by misery is not well supported by history. For example, Hamilton (1978) analyzed the structural sources of adventurism using demographic data from the days of the gold rush in California. He found that gold rush entrepreneurs were primarily professionals, upper class, and young. They were not from marginal social groups. More inclusive studies of innovation (Mansfield, 1968) and revolution (Brinton, 1938) similarly suggest that risk taking is not connected to adversity in a simple way.

In sum, the two major tenets of the classical approach to risk attitudes, namely, that people are risk averse and that the correlation between risk and return is positive, do not seem to receive uniform support. Evidence suggests that people behave as both risk averse and risk seeking in different situations, confirming Slovic's (1964) argument that one cannot generalize from risk attitudes in one context to another. Hence, the classification of risk takers based on personality measures may not succeed either. Second, the belief in the positive correlation between risk and return comes from a retrospective analysis of financial markets. Yet, there have been studies showing the opposite findings, and as Ruefli (1990) noted, the ability to generalize from such findings is constrained by considerations of data, measures, and the like. Furthermore, a retrospective analysis does not guarantee that investor behavior facing risky choices on future returns would eventually conform to it. Finally, the situation is more murky in cases where financial data are not available.

Dealing with Risk

In conventional decision theory formulations, choice involves a trade-off between risk and expected return. Risk-averse decision makers prefer relatively low risks and are willing to sacrifice some expected return in order to reduce the variation in possible outcomes. Risk-seeking decision makers prefer relatively high risks and are willing to sacrifice some expected return in order to increase the variation. The theory assumes that decision makers deal with risks by first calculating and then choosing among the alternative risk-return combinations that are available.

It is not clear that actual decision makers treat risk in such a way. For example, Israeli defense decision makers seem to have dealt with the subject of shelter construction in a way that ignored a decision theory definition of risk (Lanir and Shapira, 1984). There are indications that decision makers sometimes deny risk, saying that there is no risk or that it is so small that it can be ignored. A common form of denial combines acceptance of the actuarial reality of the risk with refusal to associate that reality with the denier's self (Weinstein, 1980). The word *denial* suggests a psychological pathology; it may, of course, be a more philosophical rejection of the relevance of probabilistic reasoning for a single case, or it could be a belief in the causal basis of events. The tendency of individuals to perceive chance events as causal and under control has been documented in various experiments (Langer, 1975), as has the tendency to develop causal theories of events even when the relations between events are known to be only incidental (Tversky and Kahneman, 1982). Furthermore, in a recent study, Heath and Tversky (1991) demonstrated that familiarity plays a major role in risk taking. They showed that subjects were more willing to bet on an event in an area where they were self-proclaimed experts than on a random event, even though the probabilities in both cases were the same.

In sum, the classical approach makes the assumption that people are passive vis-à-vis the parameters of risk alternatives. This may be true in financial settings such as in trading on the New York Stock Exchange where the individual has no influence whatsoever on either the outcomes or the probabilities of different outcomes. However, in real life, people develop beliefs about the ability to exert control (Langer, 1975) and skill through familiarity. Although both of these notions are most likely faulty, in terms of affecting the outcomes of risky choices, they may have some explanatory power regarding investor behavior. French and Poterba (1991) examined the rather minuscule portion of portfolios that investors hold in foreign shares. This would seem to counter the notion of diversification promoted by experts who study portfolio theory. After looking at a few potential rational explanations, the two economists resorted to the familiarity argument, suggesting that the bias in portfolio allocation against foreign shares is a consequence of people's belief that they themselves (i.e., the investors) are not familiar with foreign markets.

Looking at the three aspects—the definition of risk, attitudes toward risk, and dealing with risk—one cannot avoid noticing a clear difference between the tenets of the classical approach and the ways people define risk, develop attitudes toward risk, and deal with it. Such findings call for a systematic study of these aspects as they are viewed by people who deal with risk on a frequent basis.

Part 2

MANAGERIAL PERSPECTIVES ON RISK TAKING: AN EMPIRICAL STUDY

Chapter 3

THE STUDY:
METHODS AND PARTICIPANTS

Proponents of the rational model of choice behavior tend to dismiss evidence collected by psychologists in experimental settings. They argue that such settings are artificial and that subjects' behavior can in no way reflect their behavior in actual settings, with real risks and incentives. There are clear advantages to running experiments, but it must be admitted that they lack on generalizability. One of the major criticisms of the classical approach is that risk taking is context dependent (March and Shapira, 1987). Context in this respect is the individual's focus of attention; focusing on survival or aspiration level may lead to different degrees of risk taking. Thus, it follows that one may gain by studying risk taking in realistic contexts rather than in artificial settings.

Risk is a pervasive phenomenon that we encounter on a daily basis when we cross a road, travel on a highway, or eat in an unfamiliar restaurant. It seems, however, that people seldom deliberate about such choices from the perspective of risk taking. In contrast, several groups of professionals are involved in risk taking on a regular basis, and they often deliberate about the risks involved in their choices. Such professionals include physicians, military officers, insurance officials, and managers.

Since the classical model has been developed with the notion of gambling, or making choices among a few alternatives, it appears that decisions made by managers would be closer to this metaphor than decisions made by other professionals, as both amounts and probabilities can be more easily defined. Thus, there is good reason to study managerial perspectives on risk taking. In addition, it should be noted that risk taking is an important aspect of managerial decision making, as attested to by its standing in managerial ideology (Peters and Waterman, 1982) and by the increasing interest in risk assessment and management (Yates, 1992). However, with the exception of a study by MacCrimmon and Wehrung (1986), empirical investigations of decision making in organizations have not generally focused directly on the conceptions of risk and risk taking held by managers (March, 1981a); and empirical investigations of risk in decision making have not generally focused on managerial behavior (Vlek and Stallen, 1980; Schoemaker, 1980, 1982; Slovic, Fischhoff, and Lichtenstein, 1982). As a result, the relation between decision theoretic conceptions of risk and conceptions of risk held by managers remains relatively murky. This book reports on an extensive study of risk perceptions and conceptions held by practicing managers.

METHODS FOR STUDYING RISK

There are different strategies for studying risk taking behavior. In economics a distinction is drawn between *expressed preferences* and *revealed preferences*. The former refers to attitudes and the latter to behavior. Economists are mainly interested in outcomes, so they tend to focus on behaviors. Thus, if a person invests in a portfolio that has a large element of new start-ups, the investor may be defined as behaving in a risk-seeking manner. On the other hand, if a person chooses to invest in a very conservative portfolio, she may be considered risk averse. If one looks at a person's portfolio and assumes that she chose that portfolio, one can refer to it as the person's *revealed preferences*.

On the other hand, people can be asked to express their attitudes toward risky options by, say, rating their attitudes on a scale. One end of the scale can be labeled "very risky," and the other end may be marked "not risky at all" or "very conservative." If a person chooses a point on the scale as describing his attitude, it can be said that the scale value is a measure of the person's risk preference. Psychologists often study attitudes toward risk in that manner which is labeled *expressed preferences.*

A debate may ensue as to which is a better measure of risk, the attitudinal or the behavioral. Obviously, if one measures both, there may be an advantage. Nevertheless, often the two do not coincide; that is, a person may rate an option from a set presented to her as risky, and say that it describes her attitude, but choose a conservative alternative from among the same set of options when requested to make a choice. The other phenomenon can also occur, namely, a person may express a conservative viewpoint as describing her attitudes by rating the conservative option as fitting her preference, yet choose a more risky alternative when asked to choose from among options of the same set. Examples of discrepancy among attitudes and behavior are frequent. Occasions under which they may occur have been analyzed in different contexts, such as consumer behavior.

Another dimension that may distinguish among different ways of studying risk is whether the study is done under controlled experimental conditions or in a less constrained, more real-life situation. In experimental laboratory situations one can exert *control* but one loses on generalizability and external validity. Imagine transplanting into a laboratory situation a context in which a subject (resembling an entrepreneur) has to choose an investment of $2 million. In most laboratory situations, subjects do not consider choices whose outcomes would be out of the range of losing or winning, say, $50. On the other hand, if one runs a study out of the laboratory, one has less control and cannot be certain that the variables measured are the ones that really affect choices. Furthermore, laboratory experiments are constrained in time and subjects find out about the outcomes of their choices very rapidly. In contrast, in some real decision-making situations such as in the pharmaceutical industry, it may take up to ten years to find out what the ultimate outcome is (Nichols, 1994).

In choosing a research strategy, a major issue is whether or not the question of the research can be framed as a hypothesis. In an experimental laboratory situation the researcher decides on a relatively small number of variables and controls the rest (i.e., "*ceteris paribus*"). Then, he manipulates the independent variable and observes the effects of this manipulation on the dependent variable(s). It is clear, though, that if he doesn't have a clear hypothesis that is formulated as a causal relation (i.e., Variable A affects Variable B), he won't be able to tell which variable to manipulate. It is often difficult to capture the richness of real decision-making situations in a laboratory setting. One way to infuse some aspects of real situations into the laboratory is by simulating some aspects of real decision-making settings. Some research on managerial risk taking has followed this approach (Payne, Laughhunn and Crum, 1981). If, however, the situation is such that hypotheses on causal relations cannot be formulated, an exploratory study should be conducted. Methods used in exploratory designs include doing interviews and conducting surveys. In using such methods it is hard to test hypotheses, but it is a good way to generate them and to develop research questions.

OTHER LARGE-SCALE STUDIES OF RISK TAKING

In addition to the numerous experimental laboratory studies of risk and risk perceptions, there have been major survey type studies of risk. Among them are Kunreuther et al.'s 1978 study of disaster insurance behavior and MacCrimmon and Wehrung's 1986 survey of risk taking by managers. In one of the largest studies of insurance behavior, Kunreuther et al. surveyed over 3,000 homeowners in either flood-prone or earthquake-prone areas of the United States. Their findings cast doubt on the assumption that homeowners behaved in a way that was compatible with the canons of rationality. MacCrimmon and Wehrung ran a large survey of executives' risk taking. They created what is known as an *in-basket simulation*. In such a simulation, managers are presented with several memos (resembling their basket of incoming mail) that describe several problems on which they have to take action. MacCrimmon and Wehrung mailed to several thousand executives in the United States and Canada a sixty-page questionnaire requesting responses to several hypothetical situations described in the in-basket booklet. They also asked the executives several questions about their general attitudes toward risk and requested them to make choices among different investment gambles.

There are many advantages to such a survey. In particular, all respondents answer the same questions, hence comparisons across participants are possible. However, response rates to surveys are often low, so one needs to approach a large population of potential subjects. Indeed, MacCrimmon and Wehrung (1986, p. 66) obtained 192 completed questionnaires out of 2,720 they sent by mail. This 7% response rate prompted them to call on the phone and set up interviews with 450 executives in 90 Canadian firms, where they were able to get 215 completed questionnaires (48% response rate). Their third subsample came from 85 American firms, where they received 102 completed questionnaires out of 360, for a response rate of 28%. All in all, they obtained questionnaires from 509 executives.

This survey produced data that provided the possibility of many statistical analyses and cross-respondent comparisons. The fact that all participants responded to the same situation described in the in-basket scenario may have some drawbacks. The main potential drawback is that such a scenario may miss some specifics and peculiarities of certain situations in some companies. An alternative method would be to try to interview executives in face-to-face situations and to tailor the response instrument to their specific risk taking situations. Clearly, there are drawbacks to such a method in terms of statistical analyses and cross-respondent comparisons. The potential benefits are that the researcher can get deeply into the respondent's conceptions of risk as well as her attitudes toward the real risk she faced. Since the present study focused on such questions, the latter method was selected.

THE PRESENT STUDY

The study reported here was designed as a two-stage study. In the first stage, very lengthy and detailed interviews were conducted with 50 top executives. In that stage, the objective was to conduct open-ended interviews, so as to arrive at potential determinants of risk taking that cannot be detected while using instruments such as a closed-form questionnaire. Based on the results of the interviews, a questionnaire was designed and subsequently used in obtaining responses from some 656 executives. As can be imagined, such a study may take a long time;

therefore, in the process, the responses of managers to the questions were used to revise the questionnaire. Thus, after open-ended questions yielded a pattern of responses, they were used to construct closed-form items formulated as response scales that could be used to measure responses in a more quantitative way. The process can therefore be described as a sequential modification of the open-ended interview questionnaire. The final version appears in Appendix 2.

PARTICIPANTS

The study was run in two stages. The initial sample included 10 American and 40 Israeli executives. There were 45 males and 5 females. The executives came from 20 different organizations. The American sample included the presidents of a precision instruments company and a national recording company, four senior vice presidents of high-tech corporations, a senior vice president of a brokerage company, a vice president of a large construction company, a project manager for a large aerospace corporation, and an assistant director of finance for a large liquor corporation. Their ages ranged from 32 to 60 years, and their tenure in their companies at the time of the interview ranged from 5 to 25 years. The Israeli managers included 5 presidents of high-tech corporations, the president of a venture capital firm, 3 entrepreneurs, a senior vice president of finance for a large furniture corporation, 4 colonels in the Israeli Defense Forces, a colonel in the national police central command, and 25 department managers and project managers from large, high-tech corporations. Their ages ranged from 25 to 50 years, and their tenure in their organizations at the time of the interview ranged from 4 to 18 years.

The study was exploratory in nature. The sample was not random. An effort was made to secure a broad spectrum of kinds of high-level managers and to assure that the managers participating were involved in decision making of the kind that would normally be seen as including considerations of risk. As a result of the second criterion, the sample included a much higher proportion of managers from high-tech companies than would a random sample of responsible managers.

Following the documentation and analysis of the initial sample (Shapira, 1986), data were collected from an additional sample of 656 managers. This is a very large sample, and, although the managers were not randomly selected from some population, the sample size partly compensated for this deficiency. The second sample included some 355 American and 301 Israeli managers.

Background Information

The total sample (including the initial one) consisted of 706 managers, of which 501 (71%) were males and 205 (29%) were females. The age of the executives ranged from 23 to 62, with a mean age of 35 years and a median of 33 years. Nearly half of the managers (48%) were employed by private-sector corporations, and the rest came from public-sector firms. Among the latter, 98 managers were employed by two large, regulated monopolies in Israel. A group of 30 high-ranking officers from the Israeli military took part in the study, and a group of 85 managers from one of the largest financial institutions in Israel participated as well.

The distribution of managers according to the level of their jobs in their organizations' hierarchies was as follows. Seventy-one (10%) had positions at the top of their organizations, either as presidents or the most senior vice presidents. One hundred and sixty-nine (24%) held senior management positions; 261 (37%) held middle-level managerial jobs; and 205 (29%) held low-level managerial positions.

INSTRUMENT AND PROCEDURE

The First Stage

The data in this stage were collected in interviews. The interviews were structured by a set of questions, but the main effort was to induce the respondents to talk about risk as they saw it, as well as to collect systematic "forced-choice" data. The responses, comments, and anecdotes were utilized in the construction of a questionnaire that was subsequently used in data collection in other organizations. Each interview used a structured format that requested responses to questionnaire type items, on the one hand, and allowed open-ended questions, on the other. The format of the interview questionnaire was developed in a pilot study with five executives whose data are not included in this study. The interviews varied in length from 40 minutes to 2 hours, with an average length of about 70 minutes. They were conducted during regular working hours, most often at the main work site of the executive being interviewed.

Each interview started with a request that the executive describe a recent decision that he had been involved in which entailed risk. Decisions mentioned by managers included such things as choosing a computer chip, putting a nose cover on a missile, purchasing a foreign wine company, developing a new product, making a bid for a construction company, investing in research to develop a new drug, and setting up a new company. After describing the decision, the manager was asked to describe its risky aspects. Following this part, the interview proceeded in a structured way. The manager responded to a variety of questions in three general categories.

(a) *The definition of risk* included items asking about the dimensions of risk, the relation of risk to uncertainty, and gambling and luck. Did they conceive of risk in terms of a probability distribution of all the possible outcomes, the positive outcomes only, or the negative outcomes only? Finally, the manager was asked whether specific aspects of risk (such as technological risk and market risk) could be combined into one number describing total risk.

(b) *Attitudes toward risk* asked the managers about the relation between risk and return and about risk taking in their organizations. Were there any organizational arrangements and incentives for taking risks? Could they identify risk-prone and risk-averse superiors, subordinates, and peers? What advice would they give to a young manager regarding risk taking? Were there any particular situations in which organizations should take risks or avoid taking risks?

(c) *Dealing with risk* queried the managers about the degree to which organizational risk taking can be controlled and what they did when confronted with a risky decision. Did they collect more information, avoid taking the risk, or attempt to reduce the risk? How did they treat estimates of risk given to them by others in the organization—try to modify the estimates, change the parameters, work on the estimates?

Each executive was requested to respond to all the items, and their responses were recorded. In addition, the idiosyncrasies of the manager and her organization led to the elaboration of other aspects and points of view. These open-ended data were also recorded. The interviews ended with a conversation about the role of risk taking in organizational decision making and in life in general. In this part the executives were asked about their feelings when making risky decisions and the part that risk taking played in managerial life.

Coding of responses. Many items on the interview questionnaire asked the respondent to make a choice among specific precoded responses. Items that did not allow for such responses were coded by two independent coders after a scheme was developed by the author. The rank order correlation of the two sets of coded responses was .83.

The Second Stage

The majority of the executives who participated in the second sample were contacted while they took part in executive development programs, in which a course on decision making was taught by the author. The questionnaires were distributed to the respondents before the course started. They were promised confidentiality and individual feedback. In addition, aggregate results were discussed at a later stage of the course.

The responses to the open-ended questions were again coded by two independent coders using the same scheme developed for the first stage. The correlation between the two sets of coded responses was .92. The final form of the questionnaire is presented in Appendix 2.

Types of decisions. The managers started the interviews and the questionnaire with a description of a decision they had made in the period just before responding. They could have described either a business or a personal decision. The purpose was to provide a wide-ranging sample of decisions. However, it turned out that the decisions they described could be classified into just a few categories. About 47% of the decisions described dealt with a business decision, and the other 53% dealt with personal decisions. For instance, the decision of a manager to grant a loan (if he was a loan officer) was classified as a business decision. However, if the manager's decision had to do with requesting a loan for purchasing a house for himself, it was classified as personal. In addition, a decision about whether or not to promote an employee was considered a business decision. If, however, the manager described his own deliberation or decision about a new job offered to him, this was classified as personal.

Taking another cut through the managers' decisions, it appears that 38% of the decisions dealt with financial problems (business or personal). Thirty-two percent of the decisions had to do with problems relating to nonfinancial, work-related issues (e.g., taking a new job, promoting other employees, opening a new subsidiary). The rest (30%) were dispersed among a variety of risk-related issues.

VALIDITY AND GENERALIZABILITY

Two questions can be raised about the methodology. First, did the study yield valid results, that is, did it measure what it was supposed to measure? Second, can the results be generalized to other populations of risk takers?

Validity

Many of the executives were interviewed, so one can raise the question of whether the results convey what managers "think" about risk or just what they "talk" about risk. This question is reminiscent of an old debate in the psychological methodology of verbal reports and introspection. This debate surfaced again in the 1980s, creating two camps: those who think that verbal reports are valid indicators of thought processes (e.g., Ericsson and Simon, 1980) and those who claim that people do not easily get in touch with their mental processes, thus cautioning that one should be very careful in using verbal reports to make inferences about mental processes (cf., Nisbett and Wilson, 1977). This debate is also related to the *revealed preferences* versus *expressed preferences* controversy.

The present study is by no means a test of these controversies, yet it has definitely tried to link actual decisions (revealed preferences) to attitudes (expressed preferences) and thought processes. Clearly, managers could devise nice models to describe their actual decisions, but it appears that the worry about the managerial tendency to rationalize their decisions was not founded. On the contrary, these managers, who were well acquainted with rational models of decision making, often described processes that were antagonistic to rational models. Thus, it appears that the research methodology yielded valid, rather than biased, responses.

Generalizability

Problems of generalizability can arise when either the sample is drawn from a specific population or the instrument and procedure are very specific with regard to a certain research question. It appears that neither of these potential problems materialized in this study. First, the procedure was rather open and not specific. In a sense, there could have been problems in attempting to conduct aggregate statistical analyses if careful coding had not been done. However, the way that each respondent defined risk and described her attitudes toward it eventually ended in a manageable amount of generic categories. The second potential threat, generalizing across respondents, was also rather minimal. Managers came from many and different organizations, and their ranks in the organizational hierarchy varied. There was also variance on virtually all characteristics of the sample. Finally, the problem that the open procedure posed for the statistical analyses was also rather minor. With such a large sample, issues of statistical significance are of less importance.

DATA ANALYSIS AND PRESENTATION

The data collected in this study lend themselves to both qualitative and quantitative analysis. The results on the three main facets of the study (risk definition, risk attitudes, and dealing with risk) are presented in both ways: as numerical summary statistics and as qualitative analysis. In the process of data collection, using both interviews and questionnaires, several aspects of the three main questions were dealt with by the executives in statements that provided much more insight than if these were merely tabulated in a statistical manner. The results are presented in a way that makes use of these statements, and, consequently, there are many quotes that help illustrate different ideas.

Chapter 4

THE DEFINITION OF RISK

The most common definition of risk in decision theory is the variance of the probability distribution of outcomes. The managers who participated in this study saw risk in ways that appear to be different from the definition of risk in decision theory. They showed very little inclination to equate the risk of an alternative with the variance of the probability distribution of outcomes that might follow its choice. Four aspects characterize the way managers defined risk. First, they referred primarily to the downside risk. Second, they attended more to the magnitude of possible loss than to its probability. Third, they made a sharp distinction between risk taking and gambling, and fourth, they showed very little desire to reduce risk to a single quantifiable construct. These four aspects are described in detail.

DOWNSIDE RISK

Risky choice implies, in theory, that one can either gain or lose by selecting a particular alternative. Although managers in this study were fully aware of this definition, they did not treat uncertainty about positive outcomes as an important aspect of risk. Although the chances for gain are of primary significance in assessing the attractiveness of alternatives, risk was seen as associated with the negative outcome. Managers were asked the following three-part question: Do you think of risk in terms of the distribution of all possible outcomes? Just the negative ones?

Or just the positive ones? Eighty percent of the 50 senior executives interviewed in the first study said they considered the negative ones only. As one manager stated, "I emphasize the downside portion of the outcome distribution when I think of risk." When asked to define risk, managers responded with comments such as "risk is potential loss," or "losing a client," "loss of reputation," and "not meeting a deadline." Clearly, there is persistent tension between risk as a measure on the distribution of possible outcomes following a choice (such as variance) and risk as a hazard or danger. The latter fits more closely the dictionary definition of risk that implies the threat of a very poor outcome.

RISK: PROBABILITY OR MAGNITUDE?

For these managers, risk is not primarily a probability concept. Although about half of them saw uncertainty as a factor in risk, the magnitude of possible bad outcomes seemed more salient to them. In describing the relationship between risk and uncertainty, a project manager for a large software firm observed, "There is a definite relationship between risk and uncertainty: The higher the uncertainty, the less likely one is to take a risk. But, one cannot forget the potential outcomes or stakes in risk taking; they have a greater level of influence on the risk taker than the level of uncertainty does." Many executives said that the existence of risk implies uncertainty but not necessarily vice versa. As one manager put it, "I can see situations where there may be great uncertainty but little or no risk." A vice president commented, "Risk implies that at least one possible outcome of an uncertain situation may prove to be dangerous. Uncertainty can exist between two or more positive outcomes." Another manager added, "I wouldn't say that uncertainty between two good outcomes is risky." Many managers appear to distinguish between uncertainty, which signifies the probability distribution (and hence probability of failure), and the magnitude of possible failure. In the words of a financial analyst, "Risk relates to potential loss, uncertainty relates to determining future outcomes either positive or negative." And an investment analyst commented, "Not all that is uncertain is bad."

In the minds of the executives, risk was primarily associated with a bad outcome. Ninety-five percent of the executives described risk in terms of the magnitude of financial loss, the loss of reputation, or the consequences of not meeting a target. A vice president for operations of one of the largest aerospace corporations defined risk as "not meeting the schedule." A senior vice president of a high-tech corporation in Silicon Valley defined risk as "the time it takes to get to the market." He said that he was primarily worried about the "Johnny-come-lately syndrome," meaning arriving in the market after their competitors were already there. The president of a precision instrument firm defined risk as the "potential loss of both out-of-pocket expenditures and opportunity costs." A vice president of a venture capital firm said, "the main thinking is about large amounts of money on the expenditures side."

When asked about the significance of the probability of potential loss versus the magnitude of potential loss, a majority felt that risk could be better defined in terms of the latter than in terms of the moments of the outcome distribution. This led the vice president of a venture capital firm to say, "I take large risks regarding the probability but not the amounts." And a vice president for finance reported, "I don't look at the probability of success or failure but at the volume of risk." In describing the difference between risk taking and gambling, one manager said, "A gamble of $1 million in terms of success in a project is risk; however, a gamble of half a dollar is not a risk." This tendency to ignore or downplay the probability of loss, compared to the amount lost, is probably better defined as loss aversion (Kahneman and Tversky, 1982) than as risk aversion in conventional terms. In evaluating uncertain prospects, most executives asked for estimates of the "worst outcome" or the "maximum loss." From such responses, it is difficult to assess the extent to which there are considerations of "plausibility" in determining the possible exposure involved in the alternative. Nevertheless, it is clear that these managers are much more likely to use a few key values to describe their exposure than they are to compute or use summary statistics grounded in ideas of probability.

An illustration of these ideas appears in Figure 4.1. Assuming that potential outcomes are normally distributed (Figure 4.1a), the variance of the distribution is conventionally used to define risk, whereby a larger variance defines a larger risk. Therefore, the distribution marked 2 in Figure 4.1b describes a riskier choice alternative than does the distribution marked 1. The managers in this study claimed to be primarily concerned with the downside of the distribution of outcomes. This is described by Figure 4.1c. Furthermore, most managers referred to the "worst possible outcome" in defining risk. Such a definition is reflected by the tail of the distribution in Figure 4.1d, or even by a discrete value whereby the range beyond that value can be defined as the danger zone.

It is worthwhile noting that these managers were well aware of the positive side of the distribution of possible outcomes. Furthermore, most of them were well aware of notions of distribution and probability. Their responses implied that, when considering risky choices, they first attended to the "worst possible outcome." Only if this negative outcome was tolerable did they consider the alternative and eventually looked at the possible opportunities involved in making the decision. Such a procedure is by no means irrational, but it suggests a different mode of approaching risk. It differs from the consideration of expected value and variance, which are the cornerstones of classic decision theory. These managers' responses are reminiscent of the idea of semi-variance as depicting risk. Such an idea was proposed earlier by Markowitz (1959), yet he found that variance was more elegant mathematically to describe the mean-variance principle. His approach, though, was normative rather than descriptive.

RISK TAKING CONTROL AND SKILLS

The managers made a sharp distinction between risk taking and gambling. They acknowledged that risk is related to uncertainty (60% said that risk is strongly related, and 40% said it is sometimes related, to uncertainty), yet indicated that risk was different from concepts related to uncertainty. Fifty percent of the managers said that the concept of chance does not describe risk, and 60% of them said luck doesn't describe risk. Only 30% of the managers said there was a strong relation between gambling

Figure 4.1 Variances and risk.

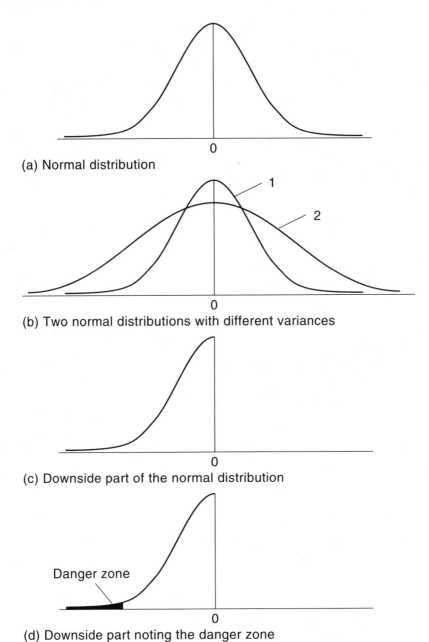

(a) Normal distribution

(b) Two normal distributions with different variances

(c) Downside part of the normal distribution

(d) Downside part noting the danger zone

and risk taking in managerial decision making, and an even smaller percentage (13%) acknowledged a relation between risk taking and playing with dice. In the words of a securities analyst, "Luck is a meaningless concept with regard to managerial decision making."

These results may be perceived to be a little puzzling, as chance, luck, and gambling are seen to be strongly related to uncertainty. The answer to that puzzle lies in the executives' perception that managerial risk taking is an endeavor where a manager can use his *judgment*, exert *control*, and utilize *skills*. When asked about the degree to which they were able to exert control and use their skills in gambling, on the one hand, and in managerial risk taking, on the other, the differences were highly significant. Using skills and exerting control were defined as characteristics of risk taking but not of gambling (see Table 4.1).

Risk taking is conceived of by managers differently from the other concepts mentioned. In responding to a question on the similarity between risk taking and playing with dice, a vice president of one of the largest investment banking firms said, "No, they are not similar. You are talking about playing with the

Table 4.1 Degree to which one can apply control and use skills in gambling and in risk taking (mean responses).

Mode Domain	Gambling	Risk Taking in Managerial Decision Making
Control*	2.05	3.77
Use of Skills**	2.23	4.37

*1	2	3	4	5
Absolutely No Control	No Control	Neither Control Nor No Control	Control	Absolute Control

**1	2	3	4	5
Always Luck	Mainly Luck	Neither Skill Nor Luck	Mainly Use of Skills	Considerable Use of Skills

odds, and it does not involve any individual judgment call." Another manager, responding to further probing about the similarity between gambling and risk taking, said, "Once again, gambling contains the elements of uncertainty and positive or negative outcomes. However, managerial decision making is based on an educated guess of what is most likely to happen and what can be done to remedy a negative outcome. That is, decision making is a continuous process in which each decision is depending on previous decisions. Gambling has only two outcomes: win or lose, and each decision and outcome is independent of others." Another manager added, "Risk is calculable uncertainty, which can be manipulated by the person involved with the situation." In the words of one vice president, "Risk, unlike uncertainty, is manageable." This feature of risk, its manageability, is the very nature of the executives' work where they apply their skills and achieve control of the situation.

Part of the emphasis on control and skills reflects the fact that many managerial decisions are dynamic and done in situations that may change rapidly. The statements just quoted suggest that the managers may acknowledge the rules of statistical decision theory as applicable to one-shot decision-making situations that are frequently repeated. They feel that the value of such rules is less prominent in dynamic situations that do not repeat themselves.

One could expect to find differences in risk definitions for managers coming from different organizations. Yet, as shown in Table 4.2, there were hardly any noticeable differences in the managers' responses. The managers in the executive program rated risk taking as more similar to gambling, in comparison with the three other groups, but their rating was still low. Perhaps they were a bit influenced by the program they were in, which used the gambling metaphor to teach decision making. All groups saw risk taking, unlike gambling, as basically an endeavor where a person can use skills and exert control.

THE QUANTIFICATION OF RISK

Most of the executives said that risk was multidimensional. A senior vice president for a large construction company argued

Table 4.2 Mean responses of managers in different organizations on the relations among risk, gambling, control, and skills.

Sample Response	Government Employees ($N = 61$)	State-owned Corporations ($N = 98$)	Financial Institution ($N = 85$)	Leading Executive Program ($N = 66$)
Risk Taking Related to Gambling*	1.85	1.94	1.79	2.56
Control in Risk Taking (Gambling)**	3.87 (2.42)	3.89 (1.96)	3.78 (2.68)	3.79 (2.14)
Use of Skills in Risk Taking (Gambling)***	4.61 (2.08)	4.29 (2.30)	4.60 (2.93)	4.27 (2.67)

Notes: Numbers in parentheses refer to questions about gambling.

*1	2	3	4	5
No Relation	Some Relation	Relation	Strong Relation	Virtually the Same

**1	2	3	4	5
Absolutely No Control	No Control	Neither Control Nor No Control	Control	Absolute Control

***1	2	3	4	5
Always Luck	Mainly Luck	Neither Skill Nor Luck	Mainly Use of Skills	Considerable Use of Skills

that, in making lump sum bids in his business, the following dimensions of risk should be considered: labor, weather, subcontractors, soil conditions, interest rates, and the economy at large. A vice president for operations in a large aerospace corporation mentioned a few other risk dimensions with regard to the construction of a particular part of a missile. Engineering aspects of risk, according to him, included cost, technical, and scheduling. He added that business risk was the time it took to get a product into the market.

If risk is multidimensional, it may be difficult to arrive at decisions if those multidimensional aspects are not transformed into some common measure. Many managers suggested that risk can be calculated. As one marketing manager said, "Risk, unlike uncertainty, can be calculated and estimated." If this means that the calculation can end up with one number, does this imply that it happens in actual decisions? Apparently not. Although quantities were used in discussing risk, and managers tend to seek precision in estimating risk, most showed little desire to reduce risk to a single quantifiable construct. A vice president for finance in a large liquor corporation reported that he had prepared for several top-management meetings quantified estimates of risk dimensions; however "no one was interested in getting quantified measures." In particular he recalled one meeting where the board was considering the purchase of a subsidiary in a foreign country. He brought to the meeting numerical estimates of risk, but the board members were not interested in them. Rather, they spent most of the meeting talking about the need for "developing a sense of the volatility of the political situation in that country." The senior vice president of the construction company observed, "You don't quantify the risk, but you have to be able to feel it." He then added, "You don't have to add all the risks to get one number."

Recognizing that there are financial, technical, marketing, production, and other aspects of risk, a majority of the respondents felt that risk could not be captured by a single number and that quantification of risks was not an easy task. Thirty-five percent argued that there was no way to translate a multidimensional phenomenon into one number. About 20% felt that it was possible from a mathematical perspective to arrive at one number, although they commented that this was not necessarily a meaningful transformation. Yet, about 35% of the managers felt that it could be done, or rather, that it should be done. As one project manager said, "Everything should be expressed in terms of the profit (or loss) at the end of the project, shouldn't it?" Several felt that one should average the different dimensions and get an overall weighted index of risk, but, even among those who thought such a number should be produced, most reported that they didn't do it that way.

SUMMARY

The data presented in this chapter suggest that, for managers, risk is primarily conceived of as the negative side of the distribution, with more weight put on the range of negative outcomes that could potentially lead to real danger. Furthermore, the magnitude of loss is more important than its probability. Executives reject the idea that managerial risk taking is similar to gambling; rather they emphasize that in managerial risk taking one can exert control and use one's skills. Finally, the issue of the quantification of risk is complicated. Ideally, it would be an advantage for managers if risk could be described in one number. However, acknowledging the many facets of risk, most felt that transforming a multidimensional phenomenon to one number might not be adequate or helpful.

These aspects that organize managerial thinking about risk suggest that managers cogitate about risk in a certain way. It appears that the process of thinking is sequential and comprises the following steps: First, edit the distribution of outcomes into a few discrete alternatives. Examine the worst possible outcome. If it is not tolerable, drop that alternative. If it is tolerable, attend to the positive outcomes and search for one that clearly dominates the bad outcome. Such a process is different from choice that is based on calculation of expected values and variances. It reflects managers' conviction that certain unique values, such as the worst possible outcome, are more indicative of risk than the information provided by reliance on summary statistics such as moments of the outcome distribution. This suggests that managers perceive risk and react to it as if it were defined by a bimodal type distribution rather than by data described by a unimodal one such as normal distribution. In a sense, that way of thinking runs counter to statistical analysis, where the more likely outcomes get more attention. It is possible that managerial thinking about risk may be affected more by what they perceive to be the most representative piece of information. As Tversky and Kahneman (1974) showed, the use of heuristics such as representativeness may not relate in a simple way to summary statistics. These ideas are further elaborated on in Chapter 7.

Chapter 5

ATTITUDES TOWARD RISK

It is widely accepted in the classical literature on risk taking that most people are risk averse. Further, a major tenet of the classical approach to risk taking is that risk and return are positively correlated. In this chapter, managers' attitudes toward risk taking are described as they are embedded in the context of life in organizations.

GENERIC RISK TENDENCIES

Risk taking tendencies of managers vary across contexts. Among the managers interviewed, the variation across individuals is seen as resulting from incentives and experience. In keeping with much of the literature, managers thought that some people were more risk averse than others, that there were intrinsic motivational factors associated with risk and encoded as part of an individual personality (McClelland, 1961; Atkinson, 1964; Deci, 1975). They saw these differences, however, as less significant than differences produced by incentives and normative definitions of proper managerial behavior. They felt that a manager who failed to take risks should not be in the business of managing. When asked if they could identify risk-prone and risk-averse managers, the executives responded with unequivocal, clear descriptions. Risk-prone managers were described as innovative, those who "always try to make changes and improve things," "transaction oriented," and "deal makers." They were also characterized as "confident," "outgoing," "outspoken," and "achievement oriented," although "slightly messy" and also "aggressive." Some described risk-prone managers as "open mouthed" and "egocentric." In contrast, risk-averse managers were depicted as "chicken," "nervous," "unsure," "passive," "slow," "yes men," "pessimistic," "reserved," "spineless," and other pejoratives. An investment officer from a large New York bank defined risk-averse managers as those who "conscientiously complete their job tasks but do not go beyond their job duties, meticulously record all their actions to cover themselves, are defensive when questioned, and content with normal development." A vice president for another large New York City bank added, "The risk-averse manager looks at decisions almost as they would as if it were part of their own life where the law of large numbers doesn't apply. Generally, such people like order, whether it be clean desks or uncomplicated life."

A major difference between these two types of managers is the perceived speed of action and managerial style. For instance, a vice president for a large consumer products company observed "The risk-prone manager makes quick, impulsive decisions and does not choose safe solutions. He/she doesn't consult with others before taking an action. He/she is generally independent, outgoing, energetic, and quick to fire or install changes in a department." In contrast, risk-averse managers were described as "sitting forever on decisions," and "worried about the approval of others," "never make waves," and so on in this vein.

The interesting question is whether managers see risk seeking or risk aversion as leading to success in management. It appears that risk aversion may be a good recipe for staying in the same organization. A supervisor in a large insurance company observed, "risk-averse managers often have been at the same company for many years. They are not confident of their prospects in getting another job should they lose their present one." Others felt that risk-prone individuals disappeared as an individual moved up the hierarchy. In the words of a senior tax specialist in one of the big eight accounting firms, "Risk-prone managers are either very successful or very unsuccessful while risk-averse managers perform in the middle range and are neither very successful nor very unsuccessful." Some argued that, if young managers want to progress, they needed to be risk prone in order to be promoted. Finally, higher level managers felt that there was a definite need to educate new managers to the importance of risk taking. And, the inclination to encourage others to take risks increased as a manager moved up the hierarchy. How would one pursue such a recommendation? Are there ways in which organizations institutionalize the recommendation to encourage managers to take risks? Responses to these questions are described in the following section.

ORGANIZATIONAL ARRANGEMENTS REGARDING RISK TAKING

Are there formal arrangements in your organization that encourage or penalize for risk taking? This question was posed to the managers, and virtually all responded in the negative. The few who came up with arrangements basically talked about rules such as trading limits that constrain the exposure a manager can take. Thus, traders who represent investment banks on the floor of the New York Stock Exchange are limited in the amounts they can trade. In banks sometimes as many as five levels of authorization are needed for approving a large loan. A vice president for an interest rate swaps group of a large bank noted that "there are dollar limits on swap positions I can take." Naturally, there are a variety of organizational arrangements in dealing with decision making. Seventeen percent of the managers noted that they needed authorization from higher up, and 10% acknowledged that there were limits on their discretion. Another 6% said that committee approval was needed as a safeguard in risky decisions. Yet, such limits were perceived as general features of managing rather than as special arrangements to foster or inhibit risk taking. Indeed almost half of the sample (42%) argued that formal arrangements as such did not exist in their firms.

Most of the managers alluded to the consequences of successful or failed risk taking initiatives. In the words of a financial analyst, "Being the only analyst to recommend a certain stock, if you're right it singles you out as a star. If you are wrong, it won't be forgotten." Thus, there are strong results following success or failure. When asked about formal incentives and penalties relating to risk taking, the majority (58%) argued that such formal incentives did not exist, and 43% said that formal penalties did not exist. Yet, all were aware of potential implications of successful or unsuccessful risk taking. Some (15%) said bonuses could follow successful risk taking, whereas others (20%) noted the increase in a person's reputation. Unsuccessful risk taking was most clearly linked, in the executive opinions, to demotion or removal from one's job or even dismissal (32%). An executive from a large consumer goods corporation insisted that there were no penalties relating to risk taking in his firm. Perhaps the picture is such that ordinary success or failure gets no specific reaction. However, a significant and salient deviation from normal performance is likely to be rewarded if it is successful and even more likely to be penalized in the case of failure. As a vice president for a large commercial bank stated, "There are no penalties, except if you take risk and you guess wrong . . . you might get fired."

Managers recognized both the necessity and the excitement of risk taking in management, but they reported that risk taking in organizations was sustained more by personal than by organizational incentives. Managers at all levels generally pictured organizational life as inhibiting risk taking on the part of managers. As a result, and in contrast to their enthusiasm for risk taking, these respondents were mostly conservative when asked what practical advice they would give to a new manager. They did not encourage risk taking. Rather, they said things like, "Let other managers participate in your decisions," "Don't gamble," "Arrange for a blanket," "Pad yourself," and, as one manager put it, "Avoid risk taking would be my credo." This negative attitude toward individual risk taking is particularly characteristic of managers who see risk as unconnected to uncertainty, that is, as being defined in terms of the magnitude of a projected loss or gain rather than that magnitude weighted by its likelihood. Managers who had a tendency to provide conservative advice were also inclined to see risk as a projected loss.

RISK ATTITUDES AND THE NATURE OF MANAGEMENT

Despite their pessimism about organizational incentives for risk taking, or perhaps because of it, most of the managers portrayed themselves as judicious risk takers and as less risk averse than their colleagues. The executives explained their willingness to take calculated risks in terms of three powerful motivations: the importance of risk taking to management, the pleasures and pains of risk taking, and the relation between risk and return.

The Importance of Risk Taking

Most of the managers said that risk taking was essential for success in decision making. They associated risk taking more with the expectations of their jobs than with a personal predilection. They believed that risk taking was an essential component of the managerial role. In the words of a senior vice president of one firm, "If you are not willing to assume risks, go deal with another business." This link between risk taking and management is less a statement of the measurable usefulness of risk taking to managers than an affirmation of a role. As the president of an electronics firm said, "Risk taking is synonymous with decision making under uncertainty." In keeping with contemporary managerial ideology, he might have added that management is synonymous with decision making. With such a spirit, managers are inclined to show greater propensity toward risk taking when questions are framed as business decisions than when they are framed as personal decisions.

The Pleasures and Pains of Risk Taking

These managers recognized the emotional pleasures and pains of risk taking, the affective delights and thrills of danger. Risk taking involves emotions of anxiety, fear, stimulation, and joy. Many of the respondents seemed to believe that the pleasure of success was augmented by the threat of failure. One president said, "I enjoy success and don't like to fail," and the president of a venture capital firm said, "I agonize over risk." He added that often when he has to make a decision involving risk he "sleeps over it." One president said, "Satisfaction from success is directly related to the degree of risk taken." And this excitement over danger is confounded by a concomitant anticipation of mastery, the expectation that danger will be overcome.

The Relation Between Risk and Return

One of the major tenets of portfolio analysis is that risk and return are positively correlated (Sharpe, 1964). This implies that if a person wants to get a higher return, he should, on average, take higher risks. This relation has been based on evidence collected in a retrospective manner, in analyzing yields and risks of stocks. Yet, aggregate analysis shows that there may be a negative correlation between accounting measures of risk and return (Bowman, 1980; Fiegenbaum, 1990). It was intriguing, therefore, to get the executives' perspective on this subject. Thirteen percent of the executives felt that risk and return were related; another 30% felt they were conditionally related. About half of the sample (48%) felt that the two were *not* necessarily related, whereas a minority of 9% felt the two were definitely not related. Those who felt that risk and return were related added, nevertheless, "if," "but," and "it depends" to qualify this relation.

The president of a venture capital firm said, "Risk and return are correlated . . . perhaps in the New York Stock Exchange. In my business there are often no price figures, so how can one talk about a correlation?" Incidentally, this president had a doctoral degree in finance from a very respected university and had even taught as a professor of finance for many years. A financial analyst noted, "there is no higher return for increasing risks in a business where risk is inherent." The question about the relation was then framed in a different way, namely, "if you don't take risks, there will be no return" (see question F in Appendix 2). This statement drew a quick response from a senior vice president of one of the largest construction firms. He said, "The person who told you that did not prepare his homework well." He then proceeded to explain how, even in bidding for large construction projects, there were ways to ensure high returns with only minimal risk.

Several managers felt that a positive relation between risk and return might be a characteristic of financial markets but not of other markets or other businesses. An investment officer for a large New York bank said, "In general, the statement is true, however, there are instances where there is very little risk but also great potential for return. For example, in buying a savings and loans institution from the government with government guarantees." Another executive noted that the statement might be true for monetary options but not for other aspects of management. And another financial analyst, working for one for the big eight accounting firms, argued that "in accounting firms, risk is not related to return."

When probed more about the relation, several said that the positive relation between risk and return may be true for "abnormal returns" or "excess returns." In the words of another manager who responded to the statement about no risks taken meaning no return, "This statement is not true. If you don't take risks, there will be returns but they will be marginal. Without risks, no 'home-runs' will be hit." Another idea that surfaced was one of justification of risk taking, namely, that only with large expected returns can risk taking be justified. As one vice president put it, "You cannot justify a large risk without a large return." Most of the executives expected the choice of an alternative to be justified if large potential losses were balanced by similarly large potential gains, but they did not seem to think that they would require the expected value of a riskier alternative to be greater than that of the less risky one in order to justify choice.

RISK ATTITUDES AND THE CONTEXT OF DECISIONS

Classical approaches to decision making assume that most people are risk averse. This presumed characteristic was described in Figure 1.1. Research by Markowitz (1952) suggested that risk attitudes may vary if one considers gains versus losses. This is also one of the main features of Kahneman and Tversky's (1979) prospect theory that was described in Chapter 1. In both of these approaches the reference point provided a context for risky choice whereby risk attitudes differ if the decision maker is in the positive domain or in the loss domain. Although the treatment by Markowitz proposed a different functional form than the prospect theory of Kahneman and Tversky, both approaches assume that there is asymmetry between risk attitudes in the two domains. Thus, prospect theory predicts that, if a person behaves in a risk-averse manner in the domain of gains, she will behave in a risk-seeking manner in the domain of losses. This potential asymmetry was examined here as well.

Asymmetry of Risk Attitudes

To examine the potential asymmetries between contexts of success and failure, the executives were asked to rate the degree of risk they "would take" under the following six scenarios: great success, success, marginal success, marginal failure, failure, and considerable failure (see Figure 5.1). In addition, they were asked about the degree of risk they "should have taken" and the risks that "other managers would take" under the same six scenarios.

Figure 5.1 Risk tendencies under different scenarios.

Consider yourself in each of the following situations separately:

a. You succeeded a lot and are well above the target.

b. You succeeded and are above the target.

c. You barely succeeded and are hardly above the target.

d. You failed a little and are hardly below the target.

e. You failed and are below the target.

f. You failed considerably and are well below the target.

For each of these situations, separately indicate on the table the number that most describes the risk that you would take; you should have taken; other managers would take.

Choose numbers from the following scale:

1 = Minimum risk

2 = Definitely less than average risk

3 = A little less than average risk

4 = Average risk

5 = A little more than average risk

6 = Definitely more than average risk

7 = Maximum risk

Risk Situation	a	b	c	d	e	f
I would have taken						
I should have taken						
Other managers would take						

The results for two groups of executives are displayed in Figures 5.2 and 5.3. The degrees of risk that would have been taken are monotonically increasing within each domain (success or failure) for each of the groups (see Figures 5.2 and 5.3).

It is interesting to see, though, if people exhibit the same risk tendencies in both domains. The plots in Figures 5.2 and 5.3 seem to indicate that this may be the case. To check the underlying trend one needs to look at the correlations of these measures. To illustrate this effect consider the correlations in Tables 5.1, 5.2, and 5.3.

It is clear that risk attitudes in the neighborhood of the reference point are similar, and they become more and more asymmetric as one moves into larger degrees of success and failure. Consider the values on the diagonals in Tables 5.1, 5.2, and 5.3. The correlations are highly positive in the neighborhood of the reference point (namely the correlation between a little success and a little failure) for the three different modes (I would, I should, others would). However, when moving to the next value on the diagonal (i.e., correlation between success and failure), the correlation becomes negative, and the negative value increases for the correlation between "succeeded a lot" and "considerable failure." This pattern is the same for all three response modes. It demonstrates that people's attitudes toward risk are asymmetric between success and failure. Those who would take high risks when successful would take small risks following failure, and vice versa. This asymmetry is true for both the descriptive aspect ("I would take") and the normative aspect ("I should have taken"). It is also the trend found in managers' attributions of risk tendencies to other managers.

Differential Risk Tendencies

One of the unavoidable consequences of presenting aggregate analysis is the masking of individual differences. From several interviews, it appeared that there was not much variation in risk tendencies when the context of success was invoked. However, there were some interestingly different statements regarding risk tendencies under the scenario of "considerable failure." To examine these differences managers were divided into three

Fig. 5.2 Risk tendencies (risks "I would have taken" as a function of past success or failure). A leading MBA program.

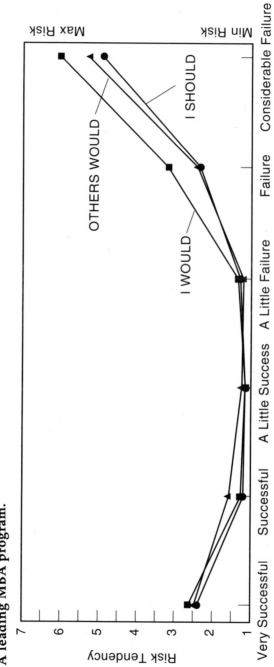

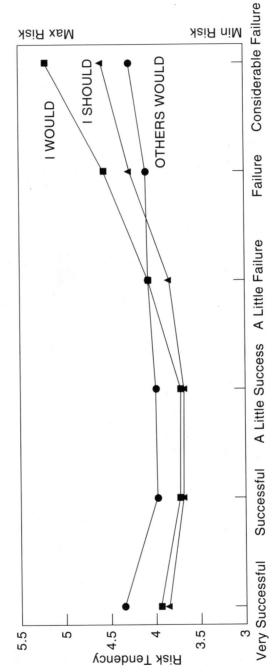

Fig. 5.3 Risk tendencies (risks "I would have taken" as a function of past success or failure). Financial institution.

64

Table 5.1 Risks "I would have taken" under different scenarios (correlations).

Failure	Success	Barely Succeeded	Succeeded	Succeeded a Lot
Failed a Little		.58	−.02	−.14
Failed		.15	−.31	−.37
Failed Considerably		.01	−.36	−.39

Table 5.2 Risks "I should have taken" under different scenarios (correlations).

Failure	Success	Barely Succeeded	Succeeded	Succeeded a Lot
Failed a Little		.57	.04	−.06
Failed		.19	−.32	−.39
Failed Considerably		.01	−.38	−.42

Table 5.3 Risks "others would take" under different scenarios (correlations).

Failure	Success	Barely Succeeded	Succeeded	Succeeded a Lot
Failed a Little		.40	−.01	−.07
Failed		.11	−.30	−.35
Failed Considerably		.01	−.33	−.37

groups on the basis of their response to the degree of risk they would take under the scenario of "considerable failure." These three groups were labeled "Cautious," "Adventurous," and "Others." The first group included those executives ($N = 165$) who said they would take *minimal* risk under considerable failure (i.e., they checked Category 1 as their response). The second group consisted of those managers ($N = 196$) who said they would take *maximum* risk under this scenario (they checked Category 7 as their response). The third group comprised the rest of the managers ($N = 295$), those who did not check one of the extreme responses for their answer. They checked a category between 2 and 6. The data are presented in Figure 5.4. The differences among the groups are greater near the extreme scenarios of "high success" and "considerable failure." In particular, the "cautious" executives were likely to take higher risks the more successful they were. The "adventurous" executives displayed almost the opposite pattern, that is, a tendency to take the highest risk under "considerable failure." The rest of the executives displayed much lower variation in risk tendencies across the different contexts. Still, the numbers displayed for the last group are a bit misleading since they are mean responses and there is variance in the responses to each category that is not displayed in the plot. Such variance does not exist (by definition) for the two other groups in their responses to the category of "considerable failure."

DECISION TARGETS AND RISK TAKING PROPENSITIES

These differential risk tendencies may indicate a basic determinant of risk attitudes. There appears to be little variation in managers' risk tendencies for situations where they have been successful. Obviously there were differences in the amounts of risk that managers claimed they would take following success, but the trends were similar (see Figures 5.2 and 5.3). The real variation comes when responding to a situation of considerable failure; some responded with caution and others responded with a tendency to take maximum risk. It is tempting to attribute these tendencies to personality differences.

Before leaping into such an explanation, it might be useful to consider the larger picture. Several of the executives who advocated taking maximum risk following considerable failure in business advocated cautious risk taking when they described their risk preferences regarding their personal lives, especially if they referred to decisions that could affect their families. Thus, the tendency to respond in either a cautious or an adventurous way to considerable failure may apply in one context such as business decisions but not in other contexts.

The differential response to the question about risk taking

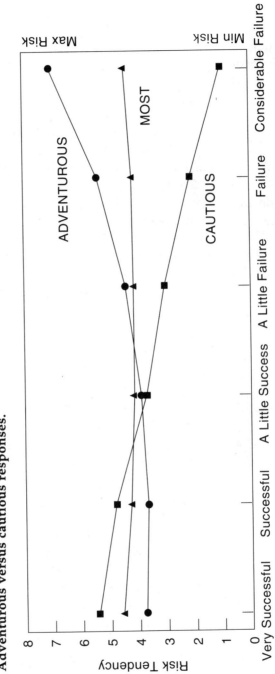

Figure 5.4 Risk tendencies (risks "I would have taken" as a function of past success or failure). Adventurous versus cautious responses.

tendencies under the context of "considerable failure" led to further probing. Executives were asked to define situations under which it would be appropriate for organizations to take risks and those conditions under which organizations should avoid taking risks (Question I in Appendix 2). All executives argued that organizations should take risks under conditions of success. They added that, under such situations, there is information and control at the hands of the executives that should lead the firms into taking risk. Conversely, the executives suggested that, under conditions of stress and failure, organizations should be very cautious about taking risks. A senior vice president argued, "I would not take a risk that would jeopardize the survival of the firm." A vice president for a large brokerage firm claimed that, in considering risky ventures, "The possible downside risk should not have a crippling effect." Another manager cautioned against risky actions "if such actions could jeopardize the continued operation of the firm." A distribution manager for a multinational corporation suggested that organizations should take risks only "if the organization can afford to bear the worst damage of the risk." Finally, a manager in a large financial firm said firms should not take risks "when it hurts shareholders . . . stopping business as a going concern. Simply don't take risks that risk almost all the capital."

Several executives noted, however, that, in dangerous situations, organizations sometimes cannot afford not to take risks because under such conditions they may be eliminated anyway. In the words of another vice president, "The times appropriate for the largest risks are at the two extremes . . . when either the organization can afford to take a risk (i.e., can afford to lose what is at risk) or when the organization is in a poor condition and cannot really lose much anyway." A project manager for a large construction company noted that situations in which organizations should take risks are those where, "either if the corporation is performing extremely well or extremely poor. In the first case, the corporation can afford to gamble and in the second, it must gamble to stay alive."

The idea that, when there is munificence, risks can be taken was echoed by a senior vice president of a large furniture firm, who said, "Logically and personally, I am willing to take a higher percentage of risk the more assets I have." This definition suggests an upward sloping segment of the person's utility function (Friedman and Savage, 1948). Such an idea is not captured by the conventional concave utility function (see Figure 1.1), but it should not be dismissed too quickly. Indeed, an analysis of the behavior of buyers of state lottery tickets suggests that there may be some validity to an upward sloping segment in utility functions (Shapira and Venezia, 1992).

When asked about what assets they insured and whether risk in personal life was different from risk taking in organizations, the main aspect of the managers' responses was the survival issue. Virtually all said they would insure only those assets that, if lost or damaged, would cause them irreplaceable loss. They further commented that most risky issues in personal and family life entailed more of these "nonreversible" risks, as compared with risk taking in organizations. Invoking this idea of the "point of survival," most opted for conservative risk taking in personal life.

The responses of the managers suggest a few ideas about the rules and mechanisms that govern risk attitudes. The managers saw themselves and other managers as exhibiting different risk preferences under different conditions. Some of this variation appears to be idiosyncratic to the details of particular situations, but there is one consistent theme: The managers believe that fewer risks should, and would, be taken when things are going well. They expect riskier choices to be made when an organization is failing. In short, risk taking is affected by the relation between current position and some critical reference point (Kahneman and Tversky, 1979).

Managerial thinking about how things are going may be organized by two comparisons. The first of these is a comparison between some performance or position (e.g., profit, liquidity, sales) and an aspiration level, or "target," for it. Most managers seemed to feel that risk taking was more warranted in the face of failure to meet targets than when targets were secure. In bad situations, risks would also be taken. Some also felt that attention to the survival of an individual as a manager was involved, that executives would take riskier actions when their own positions or jobs were threatened than when they were safe. A second comparison is between the current position of an organization and its demise. There is strong sentiment that survival

should not be risked, and that managers should avoid alternatives that may lead to ruinous loss. Most executives said they
would not take risks where failure could jeopardize the survival
of the firm, although one executive commented that "in situations where a competitor threatens the market position of the
firm, you have to take one of two risks: not surviving on the one
hand and risking new strategies on the other."

There is some obvious ambiguity in the ideas. Generally, the
argument is that a strong position leads to conservative behavior with respect to risk, so that the danger of falling below a
target is minimized. At the same time, however, the greater the
asset position relative to the target, the less the danger from any
particular amount of risk (Arrow, 1965). Recall the vice president
who said, "Logically and personally I'm willing to take more
risks the more assets I have." Conversely, performance below a
target is argued to lead to greater willingness to take risks, in
order to increase the chance of reaching the target; but the poorer
the position, the greater the danger reflected in the downside
risk. This would suggest that the value attached to alternatives
differing in risk may depend not only on whether they are
framed as gains or losses but also on which of two targets is
evoked: the success target or the survival target.

IN REVIEW

Conventional treatments of attitudes toward risk emphasized
either the curvature of a utility function or some personality
traits presumed to govern risk taking. The responses of the
managers in this study revealed a more complex picture. The
idea of risk enticed managers to talk about dangers but also
about the pleasures they derived from (ultimately successful)
risky choices they made. There may be generic risk tendencies
that are rooted in managers' beliefs; hence the clear descriptions
that were elicited in response to the questions about risk-prone
and risk-averse managers. Yet, risk propensities appear to be
affected by the context in which they are constructed and get
expressed. The term *context* should not be narrowly defined; it
may mean the organizational (versus personal) setting on the
one hand, or the more narrow context of success and failure. In

reviewing the managers' responses, it is perhaps more construc-tive to define context in terms of decision targets. Those may encompass the essence of both success and failure, as well as the larger setting in which the decision has been made. The notion of targets as guiding managerial risk taking is further developed in Chapter 7.

Chapter 6

DEALING WITH RISK

My poor mother, wise woman that she was, always used to say that no matter what happens in life there are always two possibilities. It is true, for example, right now it is a dark moment and yet, even now there are two possibilities. The Germans—either they'll come to Paris or they'll jump to England. If they don't come to Paris, that's good. But if they should come to Paris, again there are two possibilities. Either we succeed in escaping or we don't succeed. If we succeed, that's good, but if we don't there are two possibilities . . . (from Franz Werfel, *Jacobowsky and the Colonel*, 1944).

The classical approach to risk taking emphasizes the analytical calculation of risk estimates. It leads to a point where, based on calculations, risky options are either accepted or rejected. If risks are accepted, there is nothing that the risk bearer can do after the decision has been taken. In this sense risk taking is properly described by the gambling metaphor. In gambling there is no way for the gambler to affect the parameters of the gamble. Apparently, managers do not see risk taking in the same way.

Other studies of managers (Cyert and March, 1963) concluded that business managers avoid risk, rather than accept it. They avoid risk by using short-run reaction to short-run feedback rather than anticipation of future events. They avoid the risk of an uncertain environment by negotiating uncertainty-absorbing contracts. In a similar way, MacCrimmon and Wehrung (1986) found managers avoiding risks in a simulated in-basket task. They delay decisions and delegate them to others. MacCrimmon and Wehrung also found that managers were adjusting risks, and recent studies (see Bromiley and Curley, 1992; Yates and Stone, 1992) made clear the difference between choosing risks and handling risks. The picture that emerges from the current study is somewhat different. It portrays managers as *active* agents who believe that they can use their skills and exert control over decision-making situations even after the decisions have been made.

RISK IS MANAGEABLE

Several studies have suggested that managers avoid accepting risk by seeing it as subject to control. They do not accept the idea that the risks they face are inherent in their situation (Strickland, Lewicki, and Katz, 1966). Rather, they believe that risks can be reduced by using skills to control the dangers. Keyes (1985) pictured entrepreneurs and other risk takers as seeking mastery over the odds of fate, rather than simply accepting long shots. Adler (1980) distinguished among managers who were risk avoiders, risk takers, and risk makers. The last are those who not only take risks, but also try to manage and modify them. The managers interviewed in this study were similar. They believed that risk was manageable. Seventy-three percent of the respondents saw risk as controllable. As a result, they made a sharp distinction between gambling (where the odds are exogenously determined and uncontrollable) and risk taking (where skill or information can reduce the uncertainty). The situations they faced seemed to them to involve risk taking but not gambling. They reported seeking to modify risks, rather than simply accepting them, and they assumed that normally such a modification is possible. As the president of a successful high-technology company said, "In starting my company I didn't gamble; I was confident we were going to succeed." Needless to say, when I asked other executives of the same company, as well as some of their major shareholders, their opinion was rather different. They reaffirmed, however, that the president showed confidence in their success all along.

Gambling, or playing with dice, was clearly seen as different from managerial risk taking. The former requires "no decision making" and no "judgment calls." A vice president for a large brokerage firm said that "In gambling, there are specific probabilities attached to gambling odds. When you gamble, you bet on these odds. The same holds for playing with dice; you are playing with the odds, and it does not involve any individual judgment call. When you make business decisions, you use rational thinking and use your judgment." A senior vice president in another capital funding firm said, "Risk is the gap between making a decision and seeing the outcome. Risk involves variables over which you ultimately have no control. However, these can be studied so that you know the likely outcomes of cause and effect relations. You can arrange the situation so that the quantity and magnitude of the variables is minimized." Finally, the manager of a mutual funds department claimed, "In rolling dice, there is a finite combination of numbers that can occur. Unlike managerial risk taking there is (i.e., in rolling dice) no control over the outcome."

Modification of Risk Estimates

In cases where a given alternative promises a good enough return but presents an unacceptable danger, managers focus on ways to reduce the danger while retaining the gain. One simple action is to reject the estimates. Thus, only two of the senior 50 executives interviewed said they accepted risk estimates as given to them. In most cases, rejection is supplemented by efforts to revise estimates. Seventy-two percent of the managers said they tried to modify the risk descriptions, partly by securing new information, partly by attacking the problem from different perspectives. More importantly, however, they try to change the odds. Managers see themselves as taking risks, but only after modifying and working on the dangers so that they can be confident of success. Prior to a decision, they look for risk controlling strategies. Most managers believe that they can do better than is expected, even after the estimates have been revised.

The tendency not to accept estimates from others is stronger for managers who can see a clear link between risk taking and failure. As one manager put it, "I don't trust other people's estimates if it is me who has to bear the risk." Another executive added, "Never take any estimates as given," and a chief engineer for a large chemical firm said, "I'm definitely going to check the estimates since I have to suffer the adverse effects of risk taking." Finally, a trader for a large financial institution in Chicago said, "In my business I am not willing to accept risk estimates from other people."

A few executives provided other rationales for checking estimates, saying they were either expecting biased estimates from others or were planning to modify them themselves. The manager of a financial reporting department said, "I may also modify them [i.e., the estimates] after checking if I find them too tight or too loose." Another executive said, "Usually, people who are knowledgeable about a situation are also biased to some extent for one of the outcomes." Another manager claimed, "I always check to be sure that I agree with the parameters. If I don't, I will redefine the risk and modify the parameters." A manager for a major telephone company said, "I try to modify the estimates so that the risk is acceptable to my boss." An executive from a brokerage firm said, "Assuming the sources are reliable, I see no need to check or change the estimates. But if the risk estimates show high risk, I will try to change the scenario into one with less risk." Finally, an assistant treasurer for a large financial institution commented, "If I am accepting the risks (or being asked to) then I'm going to check the estimates and if possible, modify them. I'll also stoop to bending the odds ever so slightly in my favor. All to ensure that I've got the best possible chance of winning."

In sum, the reliability of the source as well as the significance of the risk involved are the major determinants of the checking and modifying of estimates. The skeptic may find comfort in an article about the numbers culture in the auditing business (Norris, 1991). Its title, "If you don't like the numbers find new ones," agrees with the managers' statements.

Modes of Dealing with Risks

The executives were asked to rank different modes of dealing with risks in the order that best fit their mode of operation. The responses are displayed in Table 6.1.The order appears to make sense, starting with collection of more information, checking of different aspects of the problem, active working on the problem, followed by delaying, avoiding taking risks, and delegating the problem. This order reflects an active mode of dealing with risks.

Table 6.1 Rank order of modes of dealing with risk.

Action*	Average Rank
Collect More Information	1.46
Check Different Aspects	2.11
Actively Work on the Problem	2.43
Delay the Decision	4.07
Avoid Taking the Risk	4.73
Delegate the Decision	5.51

*These actions were ranked in terms of the degree to which they described the way managers dealt with risk; the higher the rank, the more frequently the action was used.

It is interesting to look at the ways executives from different organizations look at these modes of operation. The responses of a sample of executives from three organizations and an executive master of business administration degree program are displayed in Table 6.2. It appears that, with the exception of government employees, who were heavily inclined to avoid taking risks, there were virtually no differences. The data show that neither delaying nor avoiding taking risks were the highest ranked options.

When asked to reflect on successful and unsuccessful risks they had taken in the past and whether the lessons were such that risk can be managed, most of the executives responded in the affirmative. An associate from a large bank said, "Risk can be managed by objectively collecting and evaluating data and by maintaining control whenever possible." A vice president for a large commercial bank said risk could be managed by "doing your homework." Virtually all agreed that financial and stock market risk could be managed by diversification and by hedging. Others added statements like, "You can modify the risks by cutting corners," "You break down the decision to small parts," and "reducing risk by restructuring the problem." A vice president for a large brokerage house said you can deal with risk by "having more and better information, and by keeping aware of situations as they change. Very important to have contingency plans if certain risky events take place." A vice president in charge of the interest rate swap group of a New York City based bank said, "I think risk can be managed at times. By gathering a

**Table 6.2 Dealing with risks:
A comparison among different organizations.**

Sample	Government Employees ($N = 61$)	State-owned Corporations ($N = 98$)	Financial Institution ($N = 85$)	Leading MBA Program ($N = 66$)
Delay Decision with Risk (Rank 1–7)[*]	2.96	3.60	3.12	4.44
Organizations Should Avoid Taking Risks[**]	6.85	4.14	4.28	3.94

[*]Other alternatives: avoid, collect more information, check problem, actively work, delay, delegate, other.

[**] 1	2	3	4	5	6	7
Only When Necessary	When There Can Be a Significant Loss	When Lacking Information or Control	When There Is Little Information and Little Control	Often	Most of the Time	Always

Note: The categorical scale is based on the managers' responses.

lot of information, following market trends, and having a loss tolerance level." This idea of setting limits was echoed in the words of the chief financial officer of a large firm, who stated, "Risk can be managed somewhat by setting targets for deadlines, revenues, expenses, etc. to the extent that targets are not decisions that should be reassessed or altered."

Taken together, there is a good deal of intelligence in these ideas, coming from executives who have experienced many risk taking situations. This experience leads to developing managers who are able to deal with risks in a more skilled manner. Consider the following statement by a vice president of financial analysis in a large New York City bank: "I believe risk can be managed. The dictionary definition of risk underscores the element of danger and hazard. These red flags should alert the risk taker to a plan of action based on the saying, 'always expect the unexpected.' The more you educate yourself to the situation, rehearse worst scene scenarios, I believe you will be better able to manage risk." A vice president for equity research marketing at a large capital funding firm concurred: "Yes, risk can be managed. Oftentimes when you are younger, you take more risks because you can afford to—you have time to catch up if the risk backfires. Each time you take a risk it is a learning process. Eventually you develop and sharpen assessment skills in risk taking! You also learn how much risk tolerance you have, and once you know that level, you can more accurately make correct decisions and trust your judgment on them. You can also learn certain methods and screening processes which help you to control the level of risk you take."

Dealing with risk is therefore a prolonged process, starting with the collection of lots of information and continuing through modification of estimates and active working on the problem. Options of delaying, avoiding, or delegating are also considered. However, experience and targets in terms of tolerance levels appear to be the best guides for risk taking.

THE BELIEF IN POSTDECISIONAL CONTROL

In classical thinking about risk taking, decision making is a particular "heroic" moment where one has to either accept or reject a risky option or choose one alternative among a few. The decision should be based on the best information and calculations. Indeed, investing in the stock market may be characterized as such a process where a decision to buy or sell a certain security has outcomes over which the decision maker has no influence. Such a situation elicits, indeed, the gambling metaphor. However, even in the world of finance, there are options of diversification and hedging by which investors can minimize anticipated failure.

The world outside of financial markets is the arena where the majority of managerial decisions are made. There, the roles of risk and return are not always clear, certainly not with respect to a single decision. Recall the president of the venture capital firm who said that in his business there are often no prices, so that it is impossible to talk about a correlation between risk and return. Recall also the senior vice president for the large West Coast construction company, who responded to the query about "no risk implies no return" by saying, "The person who told you that did not prepare his homework well." He went on to describe the process of obtaining large construction jobs. One method he liked was to arrive at a *negotiated* contract with the owner, who then pays for all expenses, and there is a markup fee. The other method, *lump sum bidding*, was far more risky because among the competitors there is always someone who's going to make an error on the bid he submits. This vice president argued (at the time of the interview) that lump sum bidding was required in the public sector, but that most private companies opted for negotiated contracts, which he described as much better since they had an element of trust in them, compared to the adversarial nature of the lump sum bidding procedure. At any rate, he said, before submitting an estimate in the construction business (by either method), "You work with the architects and engineers, and then subdivide it and ask for bidding by subcontractors. What you want is to eliminate the unknowns such as backward charging for rubbish removal, etc. Such backward charges may be as much as 1/2% to 1% of the total. So if you are talking about a $50 million project, that's a quarter to half a million dollars just there." He then continued to describe the way he could go back to the subcontractors after the deal had been agreed upon and make them change the charges if there were anticipated high costs.

This process is well known in almost any industry where there is bidding and subcontracting. If a bidder goes high for a project she may win it but suffer from the "winner's curse," namely, that her bid was accepted but she lost on the project (cf., Bazerman, 1994; Thaler, 1988). Nevertheless, as Kagel (1989) demonstrated in a study of the construction industry in Houston, often when major contractors find out that they made a mistake in bidding they go to their subcontractors and twist their arms to lower their charges so that the major contractor either doesn't bear large losses or doesn't lose at all. Clearly, although one can lower costs this way, there is no guarantee that such a process would eliminate the "curse" of competitive bidding. Indeed the three Atlantic-Richfield engineers who were the first to point out this phenomenon in the business of competitive bidding for the purpose of drilling rights in the Gulf of Mexico, Capen, Clapp, and Campbell (1971), noted that the method of competitive bidding led to losses in this business from before 1950. Before 1950, land there had been much cheaper.

Applying the same logic to mergers and acquisitions, it was shown that about a third of all acquisitions turned out to be failures and another third failed to perform up to expectations (*Wall Street Journal*, 1981b). The idea is that when managers take on a risky project, they don't think about it as a one-point-in-time decision. Rather, realizing that many things can go wrong, managers think about ways to change the course of action and to remedy potential problems after the decision has been made. As one project manager commented when she described the difference between gambling and managerial risk taking, "Once again, gambling contains the elements of uncertainty and positive or negative outcomes. However, managerial decision making is (hopefully) based on an educated guess of what is most likely to happen and what can be done to *remedy* a negative outcome. That is, decision making is a continuous process in which each decision is dependent on previous decisions. Gambling has only two outcomes—win or lose, and each decision and outcome is independent of others." Another manager stated, "Decision theory put all the emphasis on the analysis leading to the moment of choice. While it is definitely important, my experience taught me that my ability to influence whatever goes on *after* the moment of choice is perhaps even more important."

Managerial thinking about risk taking is strongly linked to the possibility of postdecisional control. Granted, the belief in control may be fraught with problems (Langer, 1975), and if one continues Jacobowsky's reasoning of a "two possibilities" decision tree (Werfel, 1944), there is a chance of a bad ending (see quote at the beginning of this chapter). Nevertheless, more often than not, managers believe in their ability to reverse errors after a decision has been made. This is what is meant by "reducing the risks," "eliminating the unknowns," and "controlling the risks." Managerial confidence in the possibilities for postdecision reduction in risk comes from an interpretation of managerial experience. Most executives feel that they have been able to better the odds in their previous decisions. Thus, it appears that managers accept risks, in part, because they do not expect that they will have to bear them.

CONTROL, SKILLS, AND EXPERTISE IN RISK TAKING

Managers develop in their careers into experienced risk takers. Through the collection of information, the restructuring of risky alternatives, and the overseeing of projects as they proceed, they develop a sense of skill in risk taking and a belief in postdecisional control. In a sense this process describes the development of expertise in management. As such, it is not different from the development of expertise in other areas where risks are taken.

Ralph Keyes (1985) conducted several interviews with individuals who talked about their experience as risk takers. One of the interviewees, the famous French wire walker Philippe Petit, said, "I don't see wire walking as risk taking. I have no room in my life for risk. You cannot be both a risk taker and a wire walker. I take absolutely no risks! I never use the word `risk.' I plan everything the most that I can. I put together with the utmost care that part of my life." He then added, "One serious accident makes you consider everything." Petit is definitely aware of the risks in his profession but he believes that he can beat the odds with training and careful planning. One of the managers used similar words when he said, "You can make profits not necessarily through risk taking but by the meticulous planning, proper calculations and good monitoring of the projects."

On December 31, 1989, the *New York Times Magazine* ran an article on cliff-hanging (see Gabriel, 1989). On the cover of the magazine there was a picture of Lynn Hill in action. At a New Year's Eve party at a friend's house, I saw someone taking the magazine and uttering the words, "Gee, that's risky." I was intrigued and asked him what was so risky, and he talked about how vulnerable cliff-hangers were, holding onto the rocks and the risk of falling down. He explained that because rocks in the Northeast were often wet, these people had very little control when climbing. I asked him whether his occupation was one that entailed risk, and he said "definitely not." It turned out that he was a pediatrician dealing with children who had AIDS. Surprised about the fact that he described his work as not risky, I said to him that this appeared to me to be an extremely risky job. He insisted that there was no risk for him because he was taking all the necessary precautions. In his words, "I don't take any risks at my work. I carefully plan everything, I wear gloves all the time, I dispose of syringes with care and ultimately there are no risks in my job." Dealing with risk apparently does not differ across professions in a generic sense. Professionals and managers alike are confident that, by using their skills to control the situation, they eliminate the risks. Their past experience has apparently boosted their confidence (which may be erroneous, of course) in their expertise in risk taking.

It is possible, of course, that these descriptions of risk denial are strategic in nature. Perhaps they are an indication of self-deception or wishful thinking on the part of the players. However, as these notions of postdecisional control were repeated again and again by most of the respondents, they are clearly an integral part of the arsenal with which managers deal with risk. Even if there is some element of self-deception, the arguments should not be brushed away. After all, would anyone suggest that a better mental preparation for Philippe Petit would be to flip a coin and decide by the outcome if he is going to walk the wire? In the face of uncertainty, a belief in one's ability to control the odds of fate may have some functional aspects, even if, on average, the person's belief would be at odds with the relevant statistics.

CONCLUSION

Perhaps the most striking difference between the classical decision theory's approach to risk and the responses of the managers in this study is the activity-passivity dimension. Statistical decision theory provides techniques to evaluate risky alternatives, but its task is often fulfilled at the moment of choice. The managers in this study could not have disagreed in a more pronounced way with this aspect of decision theory. For them, risk taking is a continuous process in which they apply their skills and exert control. Thus, ways of remedying an unsuccessful outcome become more important than any given choice at a single point in time. Although the ultimate statistical analysis may point to the aggregate picture over many choices, outcomes, and projects, managers operate on a much smaller scale (regarding the requirements for statistical analysis). Their experience has shown them that, by applying several methods, such as modifying estimates, cutting corners, and putting pressure on subcontractors, they were able to change the odds in their favor. Much like in other professions, this experience in its specific domain may give rise to the notion of and belief in expertise in managerial risk taking.

Part 3

IMPLICATIONS FOR DECISION MAKING

Chapter 7

COGNITIVE ASPECTS OF RISK TAKING

In the classical theory of choice, risk is defined as the variance of the distribution of the choice-potential outcomes. The notion of volatility is central to the analysis of financial markets. The Dow Jones Industrials Index fluctuates up and down, and its movements are considered an indication of risk. The other measure of risk used in financial theory is the beta coefficient as proposed in the capital asset pricing model (Sharpe, 1964). It measures the degree of volatility of a particular stock or portfolio relative to the market portfolio. This volatility is called *systematic risk*. The residual fluctuations in the price of the particular stock (in a statistical regression sense) are defined as residual, nonsystematic, or specific risk. In recent studies of financial markets, researchers tried to break down risk even further. Thus, Fama and French (1993) identified five risk factors relating to stocks and bonds. Among them were three stock market factors including an overall market factor, and factors relating to firm size and book-to-market equity. The two bond market factors are related to maturity and default risks. The authors present analyses of market data showing that these five factors explain average returns.

These risk conceptions in the theory of finance basically define risk in terms of uncertainty and fluctuations and deal with the entire probability distribution of the outcomes. However, as was shown in Chapter 4, managers conceive of risk as the amount of money, reputation, or market share that is at jeopardy, given choice under uncertainty. It is therefore the negative part of the distribution or even the extreme lowest part of it that signifies risk for them. Although there is a probability associated with these potential losses, it is the amount rather than the probability that looms large. Recall the senior vice president who said, "I take large risks regarding the probability but not the amounts." Another senior vice president added, "I put a constraint on the money, in most cases the probability of success is bounded from above." These statements point to pervasive features of managerial treatment of risk that deviate from simple conceptions of risk and are important for understanding managerial decision making.

INSENSITIVITY OF RISK TAKING TO PROBABILITY MEASURES

There is evidence in the present study, as well as in others (Fischhoff, et al., 1981; Kunreuther et al., 1978; Slovic, 1967), that individuals do not understand, do not trust, or simply do not much use precise probability estimates. Crude characterizations of likelihoods are used to exclude certain possibilities from entering the decision calculus. Possible outcomes with very low probabilities seem to be ignored, regardless of their potential significance. Where low prior probability is combined with high consequence, as in the case of unexpected major disasters or unanticipated major discoveries, the practice of excluding very low probability events from consideration makes a difference. In a world in which there is a very large number of very low probability–very high consequence possible events, it is hard to see how an organization can reasonably consider all of them. But if, as seems likely, *some* particular very low probability–high consequence events are certain to occur, the organization is placed in the position of preparing for a world (where low probability–high consequence events do not occur) that is not going to be realized. It is, of course, not necessarily a given that there is an attractive solution to this dilemma, regardless of the treatment of probability estimates; but the practice of ignoring very low probability events has the effect of leaving organizations persistently surprised by, and unprepared for, realized events that initially had very low probabilities.

It is possible that when probabilities are very small, the events associated with them are not perceived as random, and hence a belief may develop that events are subject to control. A marketing manager, for instance, defined gamble as a choice where "things could go either way, 50–50." There appears to be some "abnormality" in people's treatment of very low probabilities. On the one hand, they ignore them, but at other times, if the consequences are of catastrophic magnitude and irreversible as well, they treat them as if they were certain to occur. For instance, in the aftermath of the Three Mile Island accident, utility companies were not able to convince the American public that nuclear plants were a worthwhile investment, regardless of their pervasive and safe use in countries such as France. On the other hand, if people feel that they may exert control to alleviate potential risks, they may dismiss them, as was the case with the tendency not to use seat belts while driving, before using them became a law.

RISK TAKING AND EXPECTED VALUES

Statistical decision theory states that central tendency measures are the better indicators of the phenomenon described by a probability distribution. Of these, expected value is mostly recommended when continuous variables are considered. Expected value is the first moment of a distribution, and variance is the second moment of a distribution. Knowing these two moments is sufficient for a good characterization of the distribution. Indeed, some authors discussed risk taking in terms of the two moments of the distribution (see Coombs and Lehner, 1981; Payne, 1973; Slovic, 1975), demonstrating that the attractiveness of gambles with the same expected value can be altered when the variance changes. It is intriguing to see whether expected value, which is a good summary statistic, is perceived as characterizing risk for managers. Consider the two gambles presented in Figure 7.1, both of which have the same expected value of –$9.

In the interviews, these two gambles were presented to the executives, and they were asked which was more risky. There was not one executive who said that Gamble A was riskier, or even one who said both were of the same level of risk. Several of them indicated voluntarily that the expected value of both gambles was the same. However, the possibility of losing $1 million, even at such a remote chance, was perceived as riskier

Figure 7.1 Two gambles.

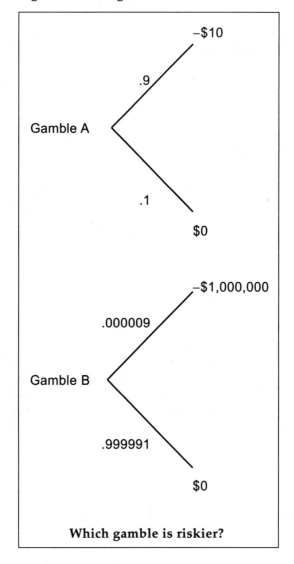

than the alternative of almost certainly losing $10. Clearly, what is being compared here are the amounts rather than the probabilities. In the words of the senior executive quoted earlier, "A gamble of one million dollars in terms of success on a project is risk. However, a gamble of half a dollar is not a risk."

It is conceivable that if a person compares gambles with less extreme probabilities, expected values play a more important role. Therefore, the author presented to a subsample of 40 executives the following two gambles, which were structured to be in line with Kahneman and Tversky's (1979) type of gamble used for developing prospect theory:

> Gamble A: 20% chance of losing $5 million
> 80% chance of losing nothing
>
> Gamble B: 25% chance of losing $4 million
> 75% chance of losing nothing

Virtually all the executives said the first gamble was riskier because it involved the potential loss of $5 million. Some added that they couldn't rely much on the differences between probability estimates of .25 and .20, arguing that these were basically the same. Half of this subsample was also presented with a variation of the prior gamble, with increased amounts, to $10 million and $8 million, keeping the same ratio, so that the expected values of the two gambles were the same:

> Gamble C: 20% chance of losing $10 million
> 80% chance of losing nothing
> Gamble D: 25% chance of losing $8 million
> 75% chance of losing nothing

All executives said the higher volume gamble was riskier, and several added that, if they treated the probabilities as reliable, they wouldn't approach such investments unless they were able to lower the probability of failure. It appears, therefore, that, although expected value does a good job of summarizing the data in a probability distribution, it doesn't provide a good handle on the way managers think about risk.

MULTIPLE DATA AND SINGLE CASES

Statistics is the science of presentation and analysis of multiple data points. Executives, however, tend to consider decisions on risky projects separately. They do not tend to aggregate over projects or situations. Kahneman and Lovallo (1993), in describing this tendency, claimed that, although managers may make bold forecasts, they make timid choices because they do not aggregate. The problem stems from two sources. First, in many cases aggregating is not easily done. Second, managers are worried that a single failure may have grave consequences despite a good "aggregate" or average record.

This tendency of managers to consider risky decisions in isolation renders the applicability of statistical inference almost worthless. This was echoed in the words of a marketing manager for a large multinational corporation when he spoke of buying insurance. He said, "When we buy insurance we make comparisons between the insurance policy and the expected damage. However, while insurance companies have multiple data points, we have only a few observations, thus our decision is very subjective." There are times when distributional data are available, yet people have a difficult time applying it to themselves. Such cases occur, for example, when a person faces major surgery. The *New York Times* reported that Michael H. Walsh, head of Tenneco, announced that he had brain cancer. The paper reported the announcement as an example of a quick disclosure, but it added that "In a defiant challenge to the odds, which say his chances are not good, he said he did not plan 'to pay any attention to statistical probability'" (*New York Times*, 1992). Obviously, that statement can be interpreted as strategic, yet it can also convey the perceived difficulty of applying statistics on the basis of multiple data to a single case. The second aspect, namely the salience of single failure regarding risk tendencies was attested to in Walter Wriston's (1986) analysis. He said "Private lenders are unlikely to forget the Middle East War, the Iranian revolution and the political turmoil in Central America. They may be expected to build those memories into credit policies."

Probability Estimates and Perceived Randomness

People's perceptions of what constitutes a random event may not conform to statistical definition (cf. Waggenar, 1972). As Tversky and Kahneman (1974) showed, people use heuristics such as representativeness that show a clear departure from a normative interpretation of randomness. Furthermore, people tend to develop causal explanations of random events, as demonstrated in the "belief in the hot hand" in basketball (Gilovich, Vallone, and Tversky, 1985).

The executives in this study showed similar inclinations. For them, gambling is probably a manifestation of a random event, especially when the probabilities of all alternatives are about equal. Flipping a fair coin is definitely a metaphor for a random event, although it may lead to the bias known as the gambler's fallacy, referring to the belief that properties of large samples should be present even in small samples. Understanding managers' notions of randomness is important for two reasons. First, there are action implications of the perception that randomness is strongly associated with a rectangular probability distribution. As a trader for a foreign bank said, "When one mentions 'gamble,' I cannot help but think of Atlantic City, where the odds offered would never be considered by a manager." Second, considering the correlation between risk and return, a necessary premise for its existence is the belief in the "invisible hand" as governing market activity. However, recent events on Wall Street may have convinced many managers that the invisible hand may at times actually belong to some high-ranking executives from some Wall Street firms.

The Role of Probability Estimates in Risk Taking

The discussion in the preceding sections demonstrated that the insensitivity to probability estimates extends beyond the case of very low probability events. Within a wide range of plausibility, it appears to be the magnitude of the value of the outcome that defines risk for managers, rather than some weighing of that magnitude by its likelihood. This is reflected in the use of terms such as *maximum exposure, opportunity*, and *worst or best case*. The behavior has consequences. It leads to a propensity to accept greater risk (in the sense of variance) when the probability distribution of possible outcomes is relatively rectangular than when there are relatively long tails.

Although it is arguable that this behavior is less intelligent than taking a fuller account of variations in likelihood, it may be useful to observe that the "confusions" of managers about risk are echoes of ambiguity in the literature on the engineering of choice. In decision theory terms, risk refers to the probabilistic uncertainty of outcomes stemming from a choice. In recent treatises on risk assessment and risk management, on the other hand, risk has increasingly become a term referring not to the *unpredictability* of outcomes but to their *costs*, particularly their costs in terms of mortality and morbidity (Douglas, 1990; Fischhoff, Watson, and Hope, 1984). Within the latter terminology, the main focus of concern has been not on variability but on defining trade-offs between a specific risk and other costs, for example, between the frequency and severity of injury and the monetary costs of safety measures. The typical style is to deal with some discrete measure of the probability distribution over adverse outcomes, rather than with its variance. Thus, "risk" becomes "hazard," the value of an extreme outcome rather than its variability; and the central insight of theories of decision making under risk—the importance of considering the whole distribution of possible outcomes—tends to become obscured in considerations of risk.

The insensitivity of managers to probability estimates may partly reflect such terminological elasticity among writers on risk and decision engineers. It may also be attributed to some realities of decision making that are not habitually noted by students of rational choice. Typically, none of the guesses of choice are easy ones. Estimating the probabilities of outcomes is difficult, as is estimating the returns to be realized. In addition, the subjective value that might be associated with such returns when they are realized is also unclear. Information is compromised by conflict of interest between the source of the information and the recipient. Because these difficulties are particularly acute in the estimation of probabilities, it is entirely sensible for a manager to conclude that the credibility of probability estimates is systematically less than is the credibility of estimates of the value of an outcome; and it is arguable that the relative credibility of estimates should affect the relative attention paid to them.

COGNITIVE REFERENCE POINTS AND RISK TAKING

The expected utility paradigm appears not to be a good description of the way these managers cogitate about risk. They acknowledge that one can describe choice under uncertainty by lotteries but reject the idea that risk taking is similar to gambling. Central tendency measures such as expected values do not appear to them to convey the essence of risky choice. Rather, discrete values that represent extreme outcomes, especially on the downside part, appear to be the anchors of their conception of risk. From statistical decision theory perspective it is the central tendency measures such as the mean plus or minus one standard deviation that conveys the needed information for a choice. For managers what is in that part of the distribution doesn't seem to convey the relevant information.

Past research has shown that experimental subjects were more sensitive to extreme values of probabilities and that they could not distinguish between probabilities ranging between roughly .3 to .7 (Shapira, 1975). Furthermore, in a study of policymakers in Israel, Kahneman, Beyth-Marom, and Lanir (1984) showed that these policymakers were not sensitive to a reduction in the probability of war from, say, 60% to 50% but were very sensitive if the probability could be reduced from 10% to 2%. These findings suggest that reference points at the extremes of a probability distribution may be perceived as more meaningful and informative than central tendency measures. In the neglect of the central part of the distribution a great deal of important information is ignored. However, if these data are considered not to be the prime source of information, neglecting them may appear natural. This description fits with Mao's (1970) findings about methods used in capital budgeting. In many firms he found that managers did not use a probabilistic framework for investment analysis. Rather, they requested three sets of figures: optimistic, pessimistic, and most likely forecasts. The last, incidentally, was not a central tendency measure but reflected a "conservative" probability of about 75% of achieving the target. Perhaps this may be linked to the managers' definition of the relation between risk and return. Most of the managers said that the statement, "If you won't take risks there will be no return," was false except when it referred to above average or very large returns. And, most of the time when managers deal with risk, they think of these events that are below and above the average.

Conceivably, the central part of the distribution of returns represents the "things as usual" mode. Thinking of taking risks triggers the manager to first look at the extreme parts of the distribution of returns and then search for some cognitive reference points that operate as anchors. In particular two reference points emerge as guiding managerial attention: an aspiration level and a survival point.

Attention and Risk Taking

Empirical studies of risk taking indicate that risk preference varies with context. Specifically, the acceptability of a risky alternative depends on the relation between the dangers and opportunities reflected in the risk and some critical aspiration levels for the decision maker. From a behavioral point of view, the contextual variation in risk taking seems to stem less from the revision of a coherent preference for risk (March, 1988b) than from a change in focus among a set of inconsistent and ambiguous preferences (March, 1978). As a result of changing fortunes or aspirations, focus is shifted away from the dangers involved in a particular alternative and toward its opportunities (Lopes, 1987, March and Shapira, 1987).

The tendency for managerial evaluations of alternatives to focus on a few key aspects of a problem at a time is a recurrent theme in the study of human problem solving. Consider, for example, the "elimination by aspects" by individual decision makers (Tversky, 1972), the "sequential attention to goals" by organizational decision makers (Cyert and March, 1963), or the "garbage can models of choice" (March and Olsen, 1976). These observations suggest that choice behavior which is normally interpreted as being driven primarily by inherent preferences and changes is susceptible to an alternative interpretation in terms of attention. Models that emphasize the sequential consideration of a relatively small number of alternatives (Simon,

1955; March and Simon, 1958), that treat slack and search as stimulated or reduced by a comparison of performance with aspirations (Cyert and March, 1963; Levinthal and March, 1981; Singh, 1986), or that highlight the significance of order of presentation and agenda effects (Cohen, March, and Olsen, 1972; Dutton, 1986; Kingdon, 1984) are all reminders that understanding action in the face of incomplete information may depend more on ideas about attention than on ideas about decision.

In many of these theories, there is a single critical focal value of attention, such as the aspiration level that divides subjective success from subjective failure. The present observations with respect to shifting focus of attention in risk seem to confirm the importance of two focal values rather than a single one (Lopes, 1987; March and Shapira, 1987, 1992). The most frequently mentioned values by the managers in this study were a target level for performance (e.g., break even) and a survival level. These two reference points categorize possible states into three: success, failure, and extinction. The addition of a focus value associated with extinction changes somewhat the predictions about risk attention (or preference) as a function of success. In general, if a person is above a performance target, the primary focus is on avoiding actions that might place her below it. The dangers of falling below the target dominate attention; the opportunities for gain are less salient. This leads to relative risk aversion on the part of successful managers, particularly those who are barely above the target. So long as the distribution of outcomes is symmetric, the dangers and the opportunities can vary; but since it is the dangers that are noticed, the opportunities are less important to the choice. For successful managers, attention to opportunities, and thus risk taking, is stimulated only when performance exceeds the target by a substantial amount.

For decision makers who are, or expect to be, below the performance target, the desire to reach the target focuses attention in a way that leads generally to risk taking. In this case, the opportunities for gain receive attention, rather than the dangers, except when nearness to the survival point evokes attention to that level. If performance is well above the survival point, the focus of attention results in a predilection for relatively high variance alternatives, thus risk-prone behavior. If performance is close to the survival point, the emphasis on high variance alternatives is moderated by a heightened awareness of their dangers.

A Model of Risk Taking

Based on these principles, a model of risk taking has been developed and is presented in Figure 7.2.* The vertical axis describes risk taking in terms of variance, and the horizontal axis depicts the risk taker's cumulated resources. The variance depends on both the amount of current resources and the history of reaching that amount. It is assumed that risk taking is driven by two simple decision rules. The first rule applies whenever cumulated resources are *above* the focal reference point: Variability is set so that the risk taken increases monotonically with distance above the reference point. This rule is a common interpretation of risk aversion in the positive near neighborhood of an aspiration level or threat of death. A specific version might make the probability of landing below the reference point equal to some fixed (and presumably relatively low) number; that is, it might make the relation between distance from the reference point and risk linear. Behavior consistent with this rule has been documented in the literature on organizations (Singh, 1986), individuals (Kahneman and Tversky, 1979), and animals (Kamil and Roitblat, 1985). This may reflect a combination of resistance to falling below the focal point and a limitation imposed on risk taking by the amount of available resources. Under this first rule, as a risk taker's resources (above a target) increase, the unreliability in tolerated outcomes becomes greater and greater.

The second decision rule applies whenever cumulated resources are *below* the focal reference point: Variability is set so that the risk taken increases monotonically with negative distance from the focal point. A specific linear version might make the probability of landing some fixed distance *above* the reference point equal to some fixed (and presumably relatively high) number. This rule provides an interpretation of risk seeking for losses. The farther current resources are below the reference point, the greater the risk required to make recovery likely (see Figure 7.2). According to the model, risk can be varied in two ways: by choosing among alterna-

*This section draws on March and Shapira (1992).

Figure 7.2 Risk as a function of cumulated resources for fixed focus of attention.

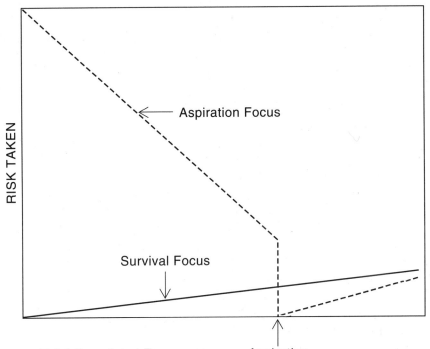

SOURCE: March, J. G., and Z. Shapira (1992). "Variable risk preferences and the focus of attention." *Psychological Review, 99*, 172-183. © 1992 by the American Psychological Association. Reprinted by permission.

tives with varying odds or by altering the scale of the investment in the chosen one, that is, by changing the *bet size*. Because the availability of the latter alternative depends on the resources available, there is a constraint on risk taking that can be quite severe as a risk taker exhausts resources. This resource constraint, however, is not explicitly dealt with in the present model.

Two target reference points are considered: an aspiration level for resources that adapts to experience (Kuhl, 1978; Lewin, et al., 1944) and a fixed survival point at which resources are exhausted. Thus, the present model differs from a strict aspiration-level conception of targets by introducing a second critical reference point, the survival point, and by assuming a shifting focus of attention between these two reference points (Lopes, 1987; March and Shapira, 1987). The two rules make risk taking behavior sensitive to (a) where a risk taker is (or expects to be) relative to an aspiration level and a survival point and (b) whether the risk taker focuses on the survival reference point or the aspiration-level reference point. Aggregate risk taking behavior in organizations is therefore affected by three processes: first, the process of the accumulation of resources; second, the way in which risk taking is perceived as success and failure; and third, the way attention is allocated between the two reference points, survival and aspiration level.

Rules such as these are commonly cited by risk takers (Bowman and Kunreuther, 1988; MacCrimmon and Wehrung, 1986; March and Shapira, 1987) and have a certain amount of theoretical appeal, but they make it easy to confuse two quite different versions of the meaning of *risk*. In the first meaning, risk is associated with variability in the probability distribution conditional on a choice. In the second meaning, risk is associated with the danger of landing below, or the chance of landing above, a focal target. The behavioral rules specified earlier keep danger or opportunity constant under changing conditions. In a sense, therefore, they are fixed-danger and fixed-opportunity rules. It should be clear, however, that any rule that keeps danger fixed as cumulated resources vary will produce variability in risk taking, and any rule that keeps risk taking (in the sense of variability) fixed will make danger variable.

Shifts in Aspiration Level

A key factor in the model is the aspiration level that determines whether an outcome is considered a success or a failure. In addition to the three processes just mentioned, a fourth factor that can affect risk taking is *shifts* in aspiration level. Consider, for instance, a person whose resource position is X_1 in Figure 7.3a. Suppose that the person were focusing on his aspiration level (marked AL_1 in Figure 7.3a) and had consequently taken a risk that had led to a successful outcome that had landed him in a new resource position marked X_2 in Figure 7.3b. The person is now above his original aspiration level, and if it stays where it was, his next risk taking action is going to be much more modest (see Figure 7.3b). However, if based on recent success, the per-

Figure 7.3 Effects of changes in aspiration level on risk taking.

7.3a

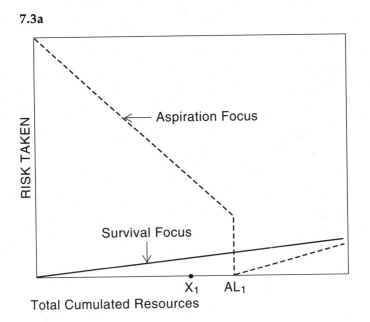

7.3b

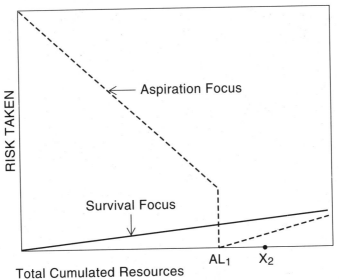

Fig. 7.3 *(continued)*

7.3c

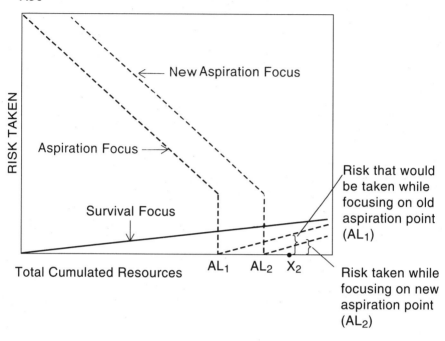

Total Cumulated Resources

son would shift his aspiration level to a new point AL_2 (see Figure 7.3c), his next attempt at risk taking would be more modest than had he not changed his aspiration level and kept it at the original point AL_1.

It is not easy to predict under what conditions people would change their aspiration levels. The impact of changing the aspiration level on risk taking is of great potential in determining risk taking in the next step. Some aspects of such changes are discussed in Chapter 8. It should be noted, however, that the notion of aspiration-level adjustment can potentially differ from adaptation level (Helson, 1964). The latter makes the assumption that people adjust their reference points rather rapidly, following new stimulation. Kahneman and Tversky, who used the concept of adaptation-level in prospect theory, noted, however, that at times people adjuest their reference points more slowly (1979, p. 286), and Thaler and Johnson (1990) documented the lingering effect of the break-even point on gambling decisions.

RISK TAKING AS A PROCESS OF CONFLICT RESOLUTION

The model examined in the previous section described two focal points of attention. The model allows for different behaviors depending on whether a person focuses on the survival point or on the aspiration target. A more complicated mode of behavior, though a more frequently used one, is described by a version of the model in which a manager shifts her focus from one point to the other. The process is a sequential one. It starts with the layout of possible outcomes of the choice alternatives. Attention is then focused on discrete values, starting with the worst possible outcome. If that outcome is not tolerable, the alternative is dropped. If it falls within the range of tolerance, a search goes on to the domain of opportunities, looking for a positive outcome that outweighs the negative one. A decision to choose a risky alternative is not done by a combination rule that integrates the two outcomes; rather it is arrived at when a positive outcome that unequivocally dominates the negative one by a safe margin is found. This is therefore a two-stage process. First, the negative outcome is examined to see if it falls within the range of tolerance. Second, if the answer is affirmative, the search goes on to the second stage. Obviously, there can be a number of iterations on this basic theme. Furthermore, if several alternatives exist, judgments of the tolerance range on the one hand, and of the dominance relation between the negative and the positive outcomes, on the other, can be modified.

One major feature of the process is the classification of outcomes and probabilities into discrete categories. The other feature is the fact that outcomes (and probabilities) are compared and are pitted one against the other. These two features run counter to classical utility theory, which makes the assumption that risky choice can be described by the use of some *combination* rule such as expected value. The sequential process described by the managers fits more recent descriptions of the processing of choice as argument-based choice (Shafir, Simonson, and Tversky, 1994), in which the manager is looking for a dominant solution (Montgomery, 1989). It also has the deliberation aspects that characterize processes of conflict resolution when two opposing perspectives are pitted against each other until one gets selected (Svenson, 1992).

Such a process may not be an easy one, and often, due to

negative correlation between the relevant attributes (e.g., correlation between risk and return), a manager may order the alternatives along the most important dimension. In most cases this may be the amount of money put at risk, that is, the downside risk. However, if two alternatives are quite similar in this respect, the manager may compare them along other dimensions such as the probability of loss. If the alternatives are similar along many dimensions, search may continue until a dimension is found that can help order the alternatives and arrive at a choice. Obviously, such a choice process may not necessarily lead to selection of the best outcome (cf. Tversky, 1972).

A major aspect of the process of risk taking is that, although managers do make decisions, they do not consider them as either the ultimate or the final point. Rather, because managers believe in postdecisional control, they are confident in their ability to remedy the decision should the situation turn bad. This belief and tendency shift the focus from the "heroic" moment of choice to monitoring of the developments along time. One of the insightful features of prospect theory was the phase of prechoice editing. In a series of experiments Kahneman and Tversky (1979) showed how people edit and frame choice problems. The picture that emerges from the current study suggests that editing is often done *after* the choice has been made. The process appears to be one of editing, choosing, and re-editing, to use prospect theory terms. Thus, managerial risk taking can be described as a prolonged process of editing and restructuring. The emphasis of the classical approach of decision making on calculation-based risky choice seems to be of less relevance in the *active* world of managerial decision making.

IN REVIEW

In the process of statistical inference, distributional data are summarized by some key statistics, prominent among them are central tendency measures such as expected value. Adding variance to expected value provides summary information based, in the case of the normal distribution, for example, on some two-thirds of the entire data. The managers focused on a few key discrete values that were not related in a simple manner to the standard summary statistics' values. The idea that these key values, in particular a survival point and an aspiration level, guide managerial attention was proposed as a basis for a model governing risk taking. The elements of the model are cumulated resources, key reference points, and a process of shifting attention from one reference point to the other. The process is dynamic and history dependent, and it allows for more complexity when the aspiration level is adjusted to reflect previous achievements. Furthermore, the process of risky choice is portrayed as a process of conflict resolution whereby the alternatives are subject to prechoice framing as well as postchoice re-editing.

Chapter 8

INCENTIVES AND RISK TAKING

The managers in this study singled out risk taking as the most important aspect in organizational decision making. Further, most of them complained that there was no coherent policy regarding the encouragement of risk taking in their organizations. If a set of rules existed, they said, these only led to inhibiting risk taking. Thus, when asked what advice they would give a new manager about taking risk, they came up with such things as "arrange for a blanket," "let others participate in your decisions," and "don't take risks." There appears to be some conflict in the managers' statements between the desired approach to risk taking and organizational practices. It is also apparent that the consequences of anticipated failure loom larger in managers' minds than those of expected success. These features of managerial risk taking are described by a model of decision under uncertainty.

In a sense, every decision a manager makes is a ruling of approval or disapproval on a certain subject. Such are decisions regarding personnel issues (to promote or not to promote a person) and decisions in financial matters (to invest or not to invest in a particular project). Considering decision making under uncertainty, managerial choices can be likened to making predictions about the future. The model portrays four possible combinations of predicted and realized outcomes: predicted success and actual success, predicted success and actual failure, predicted failure and actual failure, and finally, predicted failure and actual success. These four states characterize the possible decision-outcome relationships in managerial risk taking.

Consider a manager who is pondering about investing in a particular project. Investment decision is usually a complicated, prolonged process of gathering and processing information. The objective is to reduce the data to a small number of parameters and, finally, to a decision whether to accept or reject the project. This is done under conditions of uncertainty about future realizations that will eventually determine the degree of success or failure of the project.

When making the final accept/reject decision, the manager is faced with two major types of error. First, the manager may accept a project that should have been rejected. The other error is rejecting a project that should have been accepted. These two errors cannot be completely eliminated. Whether an error *is* made is only evident *ex-post*, after the realization of the outcome. However, a decision must be made *ex-ante*, based on available information and estimates. A major variable that affects the manager's decision is the compensation scheme that is related to the *ex-post* performance of the project.

The first type of error, of accepting an *ex-post* unsuccessful project, is usually visible (often called a "white elephant"), whereas the second type of error is often invisible. This difference in the realization of the two errors affects the compensation schemes of the decision makers and, hence, acts as a possible barrier in making a decision. A manager may weigh more heavily the first type of error than the second type, though this tendency may vary in different organizations.

This problem is more serious when evaluating research and development (R&D) projects. These are characterized by the high degree of risk, the extended investment period, and the short product life cycle (cf. Nichols, 1994). A project rejected by one company may be accepted by another firm and, hence, become visible. This can well be illustrated by the case of the Xerox copier, where the photocopying process had been explicitly rejected by a number of companies and later became a very successful, multibillion-dollar-a-year product (Andrews, 1990; Dickson and Giglierano, 1986; Kearns and Nadler, 1992).

Many times, however, an R&D project proposal is rejected and locked in the drawer and, hence, the error, if made, is invisible. Though there is usually no official estimate of the amount of rejected ideas and projects, it is likely that, for bud-

getary reasons, time constraints, and span-of-control considerations, many ideas are rejected before being given the proper
attention. Scattered evidence indicates that many of the young
entrepreneurial companies sprang from projects rejected by
large firms (Andrews, 1990; Markoff, 1991; Noyce, 1978), as was
the case with Apple Computer. Furthermore, as Scherer (1984,
pp. 222-237) noted, the relative share of innovations produced by
small firms in the U.S. economy is much larger than their relative share on several other measures, such as sales or spending
on R&D.

In classical finance, investment decision is based on the evaluation of the systematic risk of the project. The contribution of the
project to the total risk in the market is compensated for by a
required expected rate of return, which is also the appropriate
discount rate for the project. In the world of classical finance,
potential errors in decision making are ignored, for they are
diversified away in the portfolio context. Judgmental errors may
be more salient in an imperfect market or when such errors
trigger other costs for the organization, such as bankruptcy costs.
In addition, the managers responsible for making the decision
may not be indifferent to the potential errors, especially if their
compensation is related to the realized performance of the company. Such a problem can be expressed in terms of agency theory
when the manager, as an agent, decides to take actions that may
be against the interest of the principals.

A PROJECT SELECTION MODEL

The errors associated with the selection of a project are described in Figure 8.1. In the selection decision, a critical value x_c
is determined such that, if the *ex-ante* evaluation of the project
yields a value x whereby $x \geq x_c$, the project is accepted. The
project is rejected if $x < x_c$. After the decision is made the
project's performance is measured in comparison with a critical
value y_c. If the *ex-post* realized value is equal to or greater than y_c
the project is considered a success. It is classified as a failure if $y
< y_c$. The degree to which the *ex-post* realization of the project is
predicted by the selection decision is defined as the predictive
validity of the *ex-ante* evaluation and is described by the correla-

Figure 8.1 Project selection: The relation between a decision and its possible future outcomes.

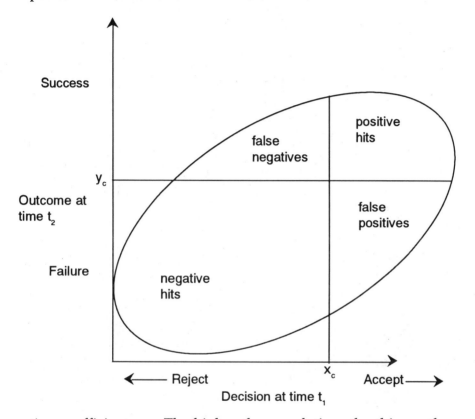

tion coefficient r_{xy} . The higher the correlation, the thinner the ellipsoid in Figure 8.1. The two extreme cases are represented by a circle (when $r_{xy} = 0$) and a straight line (when $r_{xy} = 1$).

In most cases (e.g., where $0 < r_{xy} < 1$) there are four possible action-outcome combinations as a result of an accept/reject decision. If a project is accepted (i.e., $x \geq x_c$) it can eventually succeed ($y \geq y_c$) or fail ($y < y_c$). The former action-outcome combination is called a *positive hit*, whereas the latter is called a *false positive*. If, on the other hand, a project is rejected (i.e., $x < x_c$) there are also two possibilities: If the project eventually became a success (for example in another firm) it is labeled a *false negative*, and if it eventually failed it is called a *true negative*. Looking at Figure 8.1 it is clear that a person can make two possible mistakes in an investment decision, either reject a good project or accept a bad one. These two mistakes correspond to Type I and Type II errors in statistical inference, respectively.

There are two major aspects of the model vis-à-vis investment decisions. First, for a given r_{xy} one cannot reduce the probability of one error without increasing the other. Second, in many cases, projects that are rejected don't get a chance to be funded and, thus, information about true negatives and false negatives is usually not available and therefore not visible. It should be noted, however, that although the model in Figure 8.1 describes the different errors associated with the selection of a project, in practice there may be different incentives attached to the correct or erroneous selection of a project. Thus, it is not only the probabilities of the two errors but the *utility* of the cost of each of the two errors that have an impact on managers' decisions in project selection.

It should be emphasized that, when making the decision of whether to accept or reject a project, managers do not know what the outcome of a project would be, that is, whether it would be a success or a failure. Consequently, if the project fails, the error is realized only *ex-post*. The degree of Type I error can be set in advance, based on historical data of similar projects. Granted, getting such a sample may be hard for a manager who deals with very unrelated projects. It is easier if a manager deals with similar projects and makes repeated choices.

This model has its roots in signal detection theory and it has been used by Einhorn and Hogarth (1978) to describe personnel selection. It has been employed by Galai and Shapira (1994) to analyze project selection; by Garud, Nayyar, and Shapira (1993) to explore technological foresights and oversights; and by Shapira (1993) in the analysis of risk-sharing incentive contracts.

SHIFTS OF THE DECISION CRITERION

In responding to anticipated failure, a manager who is risk averse may act by moving the decision criterion from x_c in Figure 8.1 to the right, as is marked by x_{c1} in Figure 8.2. In so doing, the manager reduces the chance of a Type I error. However, as is clear in comparing Figure 8.1 with Figure 8.2, this leads to an increment in the probability of committing a Type II error. Con-

**Figure 8.2 Raising the decision criterion:
An increase in false negatives.**

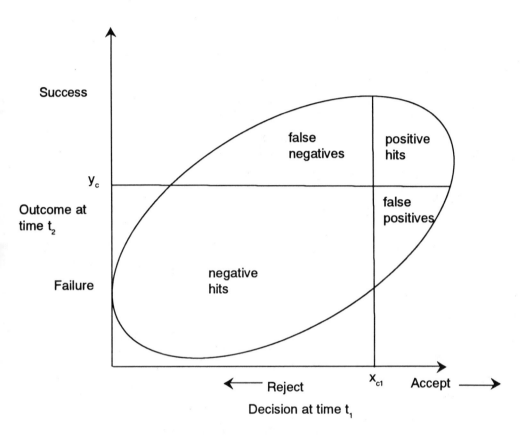

versely, a *risk-seeking* manager may move the decision criterion
to the left of x_c in Figure 8.1 to x_{c2} in Figure 8.3. Such a move
means reducing Type II error while increasing Type I error. The
point is that, by shifting the decision criterion x_c, the manager
reduces one error at the expense of increasing the other. The only
way to reduce both errors is by increasing the predictive validity
of the selection measure.

It is clear that the tendency of managers to shift the decision
criterion is strongly affected by their incentive schemes. The
more a manager is worried about the consequences of failure the
more he will shift the decision criterion to the right (described
by x_{c1} in Figure 8.2) and, hence, become more conservative. In so

**Figure 8.3 Lowering the decision criterion:
A decrease in false negatives.**

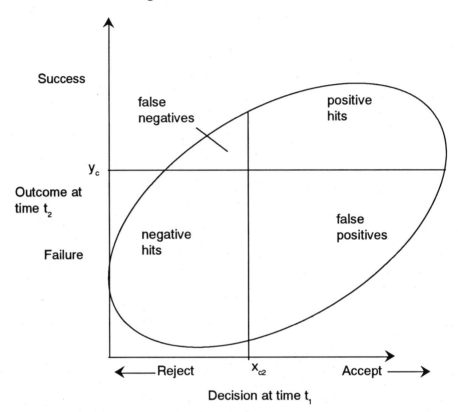

doing he inevitably raises the probability of Type II error. Alternatively, if the incentive system is more balanced, so that the rewards (and penalties) are a function of reducing both Type I and Type II errors (see, e.g., Galai and Shapira, 1994), managers may take risks in a more balanced manner.

It should be noted, however, that, although managers exercise discretion in determining the cutoff level on the criterion measure, they have no control over the outcome in terms of its success at the moment of decision. The degree of risk they are willing to take is therefore a function of the predictive validity of the decision measure, that is, a function of how well it can predict the eventual outcomes.

**Figure 8.4 Lowering the success criterion:
An increase in false negatives.**

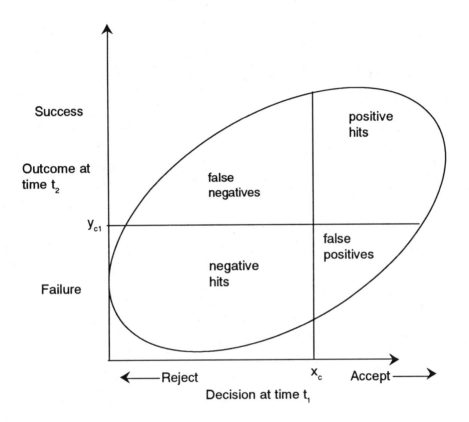

ADJUSTMENT OF ASPIRATION LEVEL

Another way of reducing Type I error is to lower the level of performance that is defined as success, that is lower the aspiration level. The effect is described by the shift of the success criterion y_c to a lower level y_{c1} (see Figure 8.4). Thus, the probability of Type I error is reduced, albeit at the expense of an increment in Type II error. Of course an opposite move, one that raises the criterion of success (or the aspiration level) is going to increase the probability of Type I error while reducing the chance of Type II error. This situation is described by the move to y_{c2} in Figure 8.5.

**Figure 8.5 Raising the success criterion:
A decrease in false negatives.**

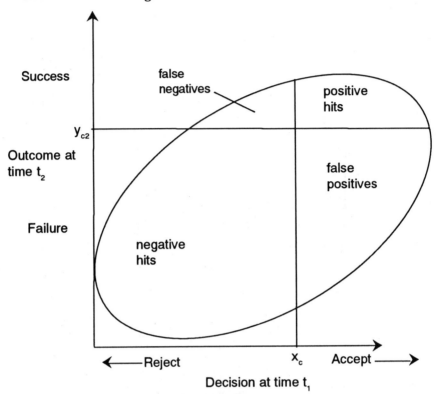

Endogenous Changes of Aspiration Level

The model that was presented in Chapter 7 suggested two focal points of attention: aspiration level and survival level. It is assumed in that model that, although the survival point doesn't change, aspiration levels adjust to reflect realized experience. According to that model, self-referential aspiration adjustment causes the aspiration level to be closer to the person's current position than it would otherwise be. This leads the person who focuses on aspiration level to take fewer risks. There may be other factors affecting the setting of aspiration levels (see, e.g., Lant, 1992), but the process of adjustment generally moves the aspiration level in line with a person's current resources. Would that be the pattern if aspirations were adjusted to reflect external effects as well?

Exogenous Effects on Aspiration Level Adjustment

Consider the following scenario. A person sets a goal of increasing the market share of a product her company is distributing to 10% from the current level of 8%. At the end of the year she achieves this target; however, she is also informed that a major competitor increased its market share from 7% to 11.5%. Does she consider this achievement a success?

This scenario indicates that performance is multidimensional and the evaluation of performance may be strongly affected by the performance of others. It is often the case, for example, that brokerage firms evaluate the performance of their managed funds relative to other brokerage firms. They can, of course, evaluate their performance against general market indicators such as the Standard & Poor's 500-Stock Index and the Dow Jones Industrial Index. It would make sense to assume that different performance criteria may be evoked contingent on the purpose of evaluation. The gist of this argument is that there can be many reference points (Kahneman, 1993) and various aspiration levels.

Managers can change the decision criteria and, by that, affect the results and the probabilities of Type I and Type II errors. However, they cannot affect the predictive validity of the decision measure by mere shifts of the cutoff level. On the other hand, changing the target, given some explanation such as unforeseen externalities, may be more handy. To that end, the multidimensional nature of performance provides a justification for evoking alternative aspiration levels, and the specific targets that get selected are heavily affected by the managers' incentive schemes. Evidence shows that managers often renegotiate targets, such as the shift of aspiration levels in the development of the Cochlear Implants project (Garud and Van de Ven, 1992).

CONTROL OVER PERFORMANCE TARGETS

A common thread in controlling an uncertain situation is, of course, the goal of eliminating the unknowns. This goal has led several managers to argue that, through the use of skills, a person ends up knowing what the outcome is going to be, even though the situation is defined as uncertain. In the words of one supervisor, "Unlike gambling where the probabilities are known but you can't do much about them, risk taking should involve ability to predict the result." This statement was echoed by many other managers. A senior manager said, "The results of decisions are usually anticipated. When managers make decisions, I feel they actually *expect* a certain outcome. Risk is the chance that a decision may not result in the outcome anticipated."

Risk was defined, by and large, as the "situation where the unexpected occurs." The continuous attempt to find ways of controlling risk and predicting the future is described in a slogan used by the Apple corporation and attributed to John Scully: "We believe that the best way to predict the future is to *invent it.*" Other managers argued that expertise in management is the degree to which an executive can restructure the problem until risk is eliminated. If restructuring can lead to less risk, then it is clear why managers distinguish between risk taking and gambling. In the latter you cannot utilize control and skills to restructure the situation.

There is however a deeper level to this argument. Consider the statement by the manager who said, "The uncertainty aspect can be different. In managerial decision making, you may be certain as to the outcome of your decision but uncertain as to the *ramifications* of your decision. In gambling, you are always uncertain as to the outcome of your decision (i.e., loss versus getting even) but usually certain of the ramifications (i.e., amount lost or won)." This manager continued, "Risk in decision making relates to the uncertainty of the consequences of your decision. These consequences could be a monetary gain or loss for you or for the company or a number of non-monetary gains or losses for either party. These non-monetary losses could be a demotion or reprimand on a personal level or a negative effect on a company's reputation. Many non-monetary losses could also cause a resulting monetary loss, such as a decrease in personal income or company profits."

The major point in these statements is that risk is a function of the ramifications of decisions. Furthermore, the manager made it quite clear that the uncertainty relates to the ramifications and not to the outcome per se. This uncertainty can arise, for instance, because of possible externalities such as the unpredicted competitor behavior outlined in the example about the manager who increased her market share. Such competitor achievement may obscure the interpretation of the attainment of a previously set target.

One way to go about minimizing the effects of such externalities is to secure consensus within the firm about what constitutes achievement, even if it is obscured by exogenous factors. This may lead to a reduction in the negative interpretation of performance, actually a reduction of the negative ramifications of the outcome. This consensus seeking to minimize the negative interpretation of decision outcomes was described by a senior vice president of a high-tech corporation in Silicon Valley who described the decision style of his president thus: "When the president has to make a decision, he runs around and asks the top managers and then decides. Actually, he 'sells' the decision and then makes his final decision according to the feedback that he gets."

MULTIPLE PROJECTS AND SINGLE FAILURES

In the theory of finance, diversification is a recommended way of achieving risk reduction, although the practice of mergers may ensue from other managerial motives (Brenner and Shapira, 1983). Kahneman and Lovallo (1993) raised the aggregation problem, asking why managers look at projects individually and not in an aggregate way. The latter is similar to diversification and may help a manager obtain a more desired degree of risk.

The picture that emerges from the current study is that the salience of a single failure looms much larger than aggregate success. In other words, although aggregate success is valuable, the occurrence of a single failure may blow success away. Thus, managers are worried about failure; they want to assure that no project stands a large chance of failing. The aggregation of projects is, of course, acknowledged, but attention is focused on each single project. Such behavior is consistent with the tendency to ignore expected values and focus on extreme values as discussed in Chapter 7.

It can be argued that this tendency may describe the behavior of middle-level managers, but should not be practiced by top management. Such an argument has its merit, yet it does not describe the actual behavior of top management. Indeed, in one of the author's interviews, there appeared a counterexample. The head of the government bonds desk in one of the largest brokerage firms in New York told the author that he has a hard time convincing top management that, in order to get higher profits, they need, from time to time, to take larger risks. He acknowledged that he can get nowhere with this argument, saying that "Top management is interested in a monotonic positive increment in the values of its funds. Higher returns coupled with volatility is out of the question even if the difference in productivity is significant." With further probing it became clear that top management is worried about its image with the investment community. Slowly but steadily increasing performance is deemed more reliable.

This policy fits nicely with investor sentiment. In discussing different measures of risks, a New York financial planner commented that the main rule for managing portfolios was that "Ninety-five percent of the clients want no more than a 10% loss" (*Wall Street Journal*, 1989). Thus, the "safety first" rule (Roy, 1952) appears to guide agents in managing portfolios. In a world governed by principal-agent relations, the agent is often risk averse, being worried about the ramifications of risky choices that turn out bad. It appears that this microcosm of principal-agent relations may be a good model to describe the relations between a middle-level manager and her boss, or the relations between top management and their principal (e.g., the major shareholders). The outcome, using Kahneman and Lovallo's (1993) term, is often *timid choices*. That is, managers behave in a risk-averse manner. In examining the consequences of this tendency, the authors pointed out that the hierarchical form of organizational decision making may aggravate the problem even further, noting that risk aversion may become even more extreme in hierarchically structured organizations.

A somewhat different example of the interface between multiple decision points and single failures is the case where multiple decisions are made on the same project. For instance, suppose that a certain amount of money has been invested in an R&D project for one year. When the project is up for renewal, there may be different perspectives as to whether it met the assigned hurdles. In such situations there are often misperceptions, as well as misrepresentations, of performance criteria, attempts to introduce new criteria, and efforts to renegotiate the criteria that had been agreed upon (Garud and Van de Ven, 1992). Such an organizational political process is not independent of incentive schemes; rather it probably reflects the ambitious goals and strategies of different decision makers, and, ultimately, these are tied to their incentive schemes, as well as to their organizational and professional reputations.

IN REVIEW

Managerial risk taking is affected by cognitive mechanisms as well as by incentives. This chapter followed the discussion of the cognitive aspects that were introduced in Chapter 7, with an added discussion of the role of incentives in relation to aspiration targets, success, and failure. The model presented in this chapter focused on aspiration targets and on the potential errors that may occur in making choices among uncertain alternatives. The asymmetry between success and failure from the incentives perspective was shown to lead to the salience of single projects rather than to the consideration of portfolios of projects. Furthermore, the tendency in organizations to focus on realized (versus potential) opportunities appears to drive managers to become risk averse, a tendency that may be heightened in hierarchical organizations and may lead to excessive risk aversion.

Chapter 9

ON THE PROSPECTS FOR IMPROVING MANAGERIAL RISK TAKING

In the previous two chapters the cognitive and motivational aspects of managerial risk taking were analyzed. The cognitive characteristics include insensitivity to probability estimates, the tendency to rely on the amounts to be lost, and the tendency to evaluate risk by focusing on critical performance targets. Consequently, the gambling metaphor appears as an inadequate description of managerial risk taking. The motivational aspect pertains to the incentives attached to success and failure. The preoccupation of managers with the ramifications of decisions and the responsibility for failure leads them to try to exert control and use their skills to restructure decision problems until they are left with minimal risk. The process is sequential and prolonged, and it is characterized by postdecisional adjustments.

A question often raised in analyzing risk taking behavior is which of the two aspects, cognitive or motivational, is more important. Take, for example, the high rate of failure among entrepreneurs who start a small business in the United States. The failure rate is as high as 95% (U. S. Small Business Administration, 1991)! Why do we still see entrepreneurs going this way if the failure rate is so high? "Because they are risk seeking" would be the *motivational-economic* response. The *cognitive-psychological* approach would come up with an alternative explanation attributing the continuous venture to this high-failing endeavor to mistakes and biases in estimation (the "it won't happen to me" syndrome).

When put into an organizational context, both the motivational and the cognitive perspectives play important roles. In organizations, decisions are often made by groups or committees or are reviewed by several managers. Although this may be advantageous, life in organizations cannot be portrayed in a naive way. Indeed, decision making in organizations is often described as a political process rather than a pure cognitive task. Furthermore, the very nature of organizations, being hierarchical systems, imputes some constraints on recommendations one can make on "desired" risk taking tendencies at different levels in the hierarchy.

As mentioned before, one can look at the hierarchical order as a series of principal-agent relationships. Using this framework, manager-subordinate relations are described as principal-agent relations, where each manager plays the role of an agent with regard to his own supervisor. The major characteristic of risk taking in that respect that emerged here is the worry of both the agent and the principal, each about his own principal. This leads to conservative behavior and a tendency to consider each project separately rather than in an aggregate manner. The ubiquitous worry about failure led managers to "think small" and not assume responsibility in a voluntary way. This makes managers behave cautiously and be on the alert for failure. As Adams (1975) has shown in analyzing survey results, a majority of high ranking officers in the U.S. Army said they were using "defensive reporting" so as to minimize the chance that they could be singled out as responsible for failure.

RISK TAKING AND RESPONSIBILITY
IN ORGANIZATIONAL DECISION MAKING

One would expect that the relation between risk taking and responsibility would be clearly defined in organizations. First, there may be legal considerations. Yet, it appears that legal considerations may not be sufficient, since they can hardly cover the variety of situations and nuances in organizational decision-making processes. As a substitute for legal considerations contractual agreements may be applied; indeed, this is the major tenet of agency theory (Alchian and Demsetz, 1972; Jensen and Meckling, 1976). If organizations were structured so that incentive contracts were the main building blocks, this might have addressed the risk and responsibility problem. However, it is clear that such contracts and/or systematic reward/penalty arrangements are *not* a standard operating procedure in many organizations (Baker, Jensen, and Murphy, 1988). Apparently, rewarding and penalizing employees is not done in a systematic way but, rather, only if a critical level of success (or failure) is reached. These critical levels may not be defined *ex ante* in a clear manner.

Information, Perception, and Sound Risk Taking in Organizations

Perception is affected by a manager's role. This finding has been known in management for many years (Dearborn and Simon, 1958). However, practical implications of this finding were seldom considered. In a study that investigated employees' beliefs about promotion decisions, it was found that the availability of information was a major factor affecting that belief system (Friedman and Shapira, 1988). In the absence of information many employees attributed promotions to organizational politics. On the other hand, when information was available, promotions were perceived to be related to merit factors such as achievement and performance. Perceptions, therefore, are strongly related to information in the context of performance evaluation.

In most cases an employment contract specifies the legal conditions under which a manager may be dismissed, including items like fraud and embezzlement of funds. Usually these provisions do not include negative performance deviations arrived at by legal actions, but by faulty judgments. The relation between risk taking and responsibility for bad outcomes is not covered by the legal aspects of employment contracts. Furthermore, even if incentive contracts are employed, most often they specify profit sharing, sometimes loss sharing, but rarely does an employment contract specify strict actions such as termination due to an *ex ante*-defined bad performance. Many managerial decisions are made in situations of risk, ambiguity, and uncertainty. These situations require good judgment, but the outcomes can be defined only up to a probability distribution. Therefore, the differences in hierarchical levels may lead to different perceptions. It can be argued that the *more* the decision-making situation is uncertain and requires judgment, the *larger* the differences in perception between an employee and her superior are likely to be regarding who is responsible for risky decisions that led to bad outcomes.

Beyond the legal layer and the incentive contract layer lies a third layer that has an effect on risk taking (and its consequences). This layer has to do with the *perceptions* and mutual *understanding* of an employee and his superior as to what constitutes sound risk taking. In particular, the more there is convergence in perceptions and understanding regarding risk taking, the clearer it will be to the employee when his superior assumes responsibility for risky decisions that turned sour and when he has to bear the consequences of such outcomes. Because management is interested in encouraging employees to take sound, risky decisions, management should address the important issue of responsibility for failure. For a good organizational design that fosters such practices, the perceptual differences between superiors and subordinates regarding responsibility for outcomes of risky decisions should be spelled out. Therefore, it appears that the *more* information is exchanged between superiors and subordinates regarding procedures of risky decision making, the less the perceptual differences regarding who assumes responsibility for the outcomes of such decisions.

Recall that about half of the managers said that there were no formal organizational arrangements regarding risk taking in their companies. Those who did report that such arrangements existed mentioned things like dollar limits on positions traders can take, authorization from above, and committee decisions. However, these regulations cannot cover all managerial decisions because exceptional situations frequently occur. Furthermore, many executives stated that assuming responsibility for failure in risky decisions was rather difficult; hence, their advice to new managers was to avoid taking risks. Is responsibility for failed decisions a characteristic of risk taking in organizations only? The managers reflected on the similarities and differences between personal and organizational risk taking.

Organizational versus Personal Risk Taking

Most of the managers said that organizational and personal risk taking were rather different. The major difference was responsibility costs. About 70% said that risk taking was easier in organizational settings. An investment analyst said that "it is easier to risk the firm's rather than your own money." She added also that "the financial cushion is larger in the corporation but the psychological cushion is greater in the family." A supervisor of traders in a large New York City bank claimed that there should be no difference between the two since "it is the same person with the same skills who is evaluating the risks." Yet, he acknowledged that in practice there are differences and provided an example: "A trader working his own account will show larger gains and losses in his firm's account than his own."

A portfolio manager voiced a similar opinion: "My employer makes thousands of similar decisions each day and thus benefits from the law of large numbers. I will live only one life. Most decisions, even if they turn negative outcomes, do not threaten the firm's viability. Most individuals are more vulnerable. Lastly, despite my education I am an emotional creature without the organizational structure to impose logic." Others also alluded to emotions, saying they feared that a nonreversible outcome could occur and that they would be responsible for it. As an assistant treasurer for a financial institution said, "In organizations one may be risking a promotion or even a job. Should failure occur, one could bounce back with a good decision or, if needed, with a new job. In family financial affairs, undue risks can have catastrophic effects. For example, investing all the family's money in stock options and losing could have much longer-lasting effects than a poor decision at work."

It appears that two elements affect managers' worry about responsibility costs: (a) whether the responsibility was for *self* or included *others* and (b) whether the negative result was *reversible* or not. Thus, most managers did not express worry about themselves but rather about dependents. Most considered family dependents, though a few said that failure in organizational risk taking may affect many families and, therefore, is more serious than personal risk taking. The second element, the issue of reversibility, is of utmost importance. Nonreversible outcomes carry enormous responsibility costs. And both elements are tied directly to the core belief of managers about risk taking: the notion of control. Nonreversible outcomes that affect others may be uncontrollable. Therefore, they carry with them unacceptable responsibility costs.

Society has tried to come up with a clear division to indicate where a conflict of interest may exist or may cloud one's judgment. Thus, surgeons are not expected to operate on members of their immediate families, and many money managers refrain from managing their relatives' portfolios. The discussion of the separation of ownership and control is central in the economics of organizations. Yet, as Sterner (1990) nicely documented in his play entitled *Other People's Money*, the question of responsibility of executives to their shareholders may be a double-edged sword. The managers in this study echoed a similar idea: Responsibility costs are a major aspect of risk taking, although they may take on different forms in personal and in organizational decision making.

IMPROVING RISK TAKING
IN MANAGERIAL DECISION MAKING

The findings reported in this book suggest a few ways in which one can talk about increasing managerial understanding of the cognitive mechanisms affecting probability estimation and the construction of appropriate incentive schemes. Yet, this endeavor may not be fruitful without looking at managerial behavior as it is embedded in the organizational culture and in a societal context.

Managerial Risk Taking and Societal Values

Managers treat risk and risk taking as important facets of their life.* They care about their reputations for risk taking and are eager to expound on their sentiments about the deficiencies of others and on the inadequacy of organizational incentives for

*This section is based on March and Shapira (1987).

making risky decisions intelligently. The rhetoric of these values is, however, decidedly two-pronged. On the one hand, risk taking is perceived as essential to innovation and success. On the other hand, risk taking is sharply distinguished from "playing the odds." A good manager is seen as taking risks but not as gambling. From the perspective of statistical decision theory, the distinction may be obscure since the idea of decision making under risk in that tradition is paradigmatically captured by a vision of betting, either against nature or against other actors. From that perspective, the choice of a particular business strategy depends on the same general considerations as the choice of a betting strategy in card games. This similarity has been recognized by decision analysts who have tried, with only a modest degree of success, to champion a criterion for evaluating managers that rewards good decisions rather than good outcomes, arguing that the determination of a proper choice should not be confounded with the chance realizations of a risky situation.

Managers differentiate risk taking from gambling primarily because the society that evaluates them does, and because their experience teaches them that they can control fate. Society values risk taking but not gambling, and what is meant by gambling is risk taking that turns out badly. From the perspective of both managers and society, the problem is to develop and maintain managerial reputations for taking good (ultimately successful) risks and avoiding bad (ultimately unsuccessful) risks, in the face of uncertainties about which might be which. This dilemma was described rather precisely by the senior vice president who said, "You have to be a risk taker, but you have to win more than you lose."

Managers often inflate the perceived riskiness of successful actions, but deliberate efforts on their part to portray themselves as risk takers are only a minor part of the story. Managerial reputations for risk taking rather than gambling are sustained by the ordinary social processes for interpreting life and getting ahead. In historical perspective, we can distinguish those who have been brilliant risk takers from those who have been unsuccessful gamblers, although the difference may have been unclear at the time they were making their decisions. Post hoc reconstruction permits history to be told in such a way that "chance," either in the sense of genuinely probabilistic phenomena or in the sense of unexplained variation, is minimized as an explanation (Fischhoff, 1975; Fischhoff and Beyth, 1975). Thus, risky choices that turn out badly are seen, after the fact, to have been mistakes. The warning signs that were ignored seem clearer than they were; the courses that were followed seem unambiguously misguided. Such reconstructions are often undertaken for the sake of finding a scapegoat for disastrous outcomes, and they end up shifting the blame from complex and unclear situations onto individual decision makers.

History not only sorts decision makers into winners and losers but also interprets those differences as reflecting differences in judgment and ability. The experience of successful managers teaches them that the probabilities of life do not apply to them. Neither society nor the managers are inclined to doubt the validity of the assessment that successful managers have the skill to choose good risks and reject bad risks; thus they can solve the apparent inconsistency of social norms that demand both risk taking and guaranteed success. Practicing (and successful) managers believe, and their experience appears to have told them, that they can change the odds, that what appears to be a probabilistic process can usually be controlled. They tend to think that way even though they acknowledge failures. However, the overall record of successful managers makes them somewhat more prone to accept risks than others might be. Societal policies may expedite such risk taking through the incentives they bestow on successful chief executive officers. One line of research that examines executive compensation and its relation to corporate performance has been the tournament model (Lazear and Rosen, 1981). According to this model, Chief Executive Officer (CEO) compensation is set as a prize for which executives in the company compete in a tournament-like manner. By tying CEO compensation to company performance through the distribution of stock options, shareholders attempt to control CEO risk taking tendencies and align them with their own. For these executives, management and risk taking are therefore almost the same.

Risk taking also fits the social definitions of managerial roles. Managers are expected to make things happen, to take (good) risks. Managerial ideology pictures managers as making changes, leading them to be biased in the direction of making organizational changes and others to be biased in expecting them to do so (March, 1981b). In a similar fashion, managerial ideology also portrays a good manager as being a risk taker. Managerial conceits include beliefs that it is possible at the time of a decision to tell the difference between risks with good outcomes and risks with bad outcomes, and that it is possible to manage risks so as to improve the odds of success (Keyes, 1985). Such beliefs are consistent with the prevailing expectation that decisions will ultimately lead to success.

Prospects for Changing Managerial Risk Taking

In accordance with the descriptive nature of behavioral decision theory, this study examined how executives define and react to risk, rather than how they should take risks. It appears that, not only do managers fail to follow the canons of decision theory, but also the ways they think about risk do not easily fit into classical theoretical conceptions of risk. Such observations make standard conceptions of risk, with their emphasis on trait differences among individual decision makers, problematic as bases for talking about managerial risk taking behavior. In the world of executives, probability estimates are treated as unreliable and subject to postdecision control, and considerations of trade-offs are framed by attention factors that considerably affect action. Managers look for alternatives that can be managed to meet targets, rather than merely assess or accept risks. Although they undoubtedly vary in their individual propensities to take risks, those variations are obscured by processes of selection that reduce the heterogeneity among managers and encourage them to believe in their ability to control the odds. This trend is also facilitated by systems of organizational controls and incentives that dictate risk taking behavior in significant ways, and by variations in the demand for risk taking produced by the context within which choice takes place. These factors are embedded in a managerial belief system that emphasizes the importance of risk taking to being a manager. And this belief system is also nurtured by the role of a manager as seen by society.

These aspects of managerial approaches to risk have implications not only for understanding decision making in organizations, but also for the engineering of risk taking and risk management. It is conventional in discussions of management to deplore the pattern of risk taking and decision making observed in management. Thus, despite enormous attempts to introduce methods into corporations of evaluating investment alternatives by discounted cash flows (such as net present value), professionals who deal with capital budgeting still favor inferior techniques such as pay back period calculations (Aggarwal and Gibson, 1989; Klamner, 1972; Petty, Scott, and Bird, 1975). The attempts to convince managers to use formal decision analysis in making decisions have not fared better (Brown, 1970, 1992).

Considering risk taking in organizations, individual managers are often criticized for taking too many (or too few) risks, as is management as a whole. This criticism is embedded in the larger discussion of whether society as a whole takes too much or too little risk (Fischhoff et al., 1981). The debate has been attested to by those who argue that in some aspects society is attempting to avoid risks (Aharoni, 1970) and others who argue that society is actually taking too many risks (Beck, 1992). As Kasperson et al. (1988) noted, some relatively minor risks often elicit strong public concerns, more than is warranted by the technical risk assessment. Similarly, in the medical industry, potential Type I errors appear much more salient than Type II errors. As Spencer (1993) claimed: "A regulatory bureaucracy will always tend to place avoiding risk above the taking of risks—even if this means slowing or even preventing medical breakthroughs" (p. 50).

The present observations suggest that some of the policies proposed to change risk taking may not match the situation as it is seen by managers. In the short run, if we wish to encourage, or inhibit, risk taking on the part of managers, we probably need to shape our interventions to meet the ways in which managers think. For example, it may be easier to try to modify managerial attention patterns and conceits than to try to change their beliefs about the likelihood of events or to try to induce preferences for high variance alternatives. These ideas are reinforced by statements made by executives such as the one made by a vice president who was enrolled in an executive development program at the time of the interview. He said, "I am tired of this school trying to tell me to think of risk taking in terms of probabilities." An alternative way was an ambitious attempt by the president of a high-tech corporation who circulated a memo (originally published as an advertisement in the *Wall Street Journal*, 1981a) to his employees (see below). Acknowledging the nature of the business they were in, he highlighted the sentence, saying, "Don't worry about failure. Worry about chances you miss when you don't even try."

There are possible implications for the education of managers in the longer run. The managers who participated in the present study do not follow decision theory very closely. They do not

---

Don't Be Afraid To Fail

You've failed
many times,
although you may not
remember.
You fell down
the first time
you tried to walk.
You almost drowned
the first time
you tried to
swim, didn't you?
Did you hit the
ball the first time
you swung a bat?
Heavy hitters,
the ones who hit the
most home runs,
also strike
out a lot.

R. H. Macy
failed seven
times before his
store in New York
caught on.
English novelist
John Creasey got
753 rejection slips
before he published
564 books.
Babe Ruth struck out
1330 times,
but he also hit
714 home runs. $\therefore$
Don't worry about
failure.
Worry about the
chances you miss
when you don't
even try.

A message as published in the *Wall Street Journal*. (1981). ©United Technologies Corporation, Hartford, Connecticut. Reprinted with permission.

reject the theory in an informed, reasoned way but, rather, act according to some rules and procedures that are implicitly at variance with the theory, even while acknowledging it as decision dogma. For instance, they talk about taking "calculated risks" when they actually mean taking "informed risks," that is, getting the parameters of the problem but not necessarily putting them in summary figures. This suggests that there might be solid prospects for changing managerial perspectives through training in decision theoretic approaches to risk and risk management. As noted, however, the perspectives that managers have are not simply matters of individual taste but are embedded in social norms and expectations. History and common sense both suggest that changes may be relatively slow, responding more to broad shifts in beliefs and formulations than to simple changes in the selection or training of managers. Achieving change by developing a sound theory of decision making should include the descriptive, normative, and prescriptive aspects together (Bell, Raiffa, and Tversky, 1988), as well as consideration of the larger social context in which managers operate.

MANAGERIAL INTELLIGENCE IN AN UNCERTAIN WORLD

If a program of comprehensive managerial education and social reform is to be recommended, one needs, however, to recognize the elements of intelligence in these managerial perspectives. Although there is ample evidence that the risk taking behavior of managers is often far from optimal, one may examine the extent to which the managerial beliefs and behaviors observed here are accommodations of managers to the subtle practical problems of sustaining appropriate risk taking in an uncertain world. It is not hard to show that contextually varying risk preferences, insensitivity to probabilities, and managerial illusions are intelligent under plausible conditions (Ibsen, 1884; Einhorn, 1986; March, 1988a). Experience, intuition, and good judgment are often recommended instead of mere reliance on calculations (Arnold, 1986; Davis, 1985; Menkus, 1988). Perhaps the most problematic feature of decision theory in this context is the invitation it provides to managerial *passivity*. In promoting the calculation of expectations as a response to risk, the theory poses the problem of choice in terms appropriate to decision making in an uncontrollable world, rather than in a world that is subject to control. It is not intrinsic to that framework that managers become passive with respect to modifying the probabilities they face, but the message there is very clear. In contrast, it might be preferable to have managers imagine (sometimes falsely) that they can control their fates, rather than suffer the consequences of imagining (sometimes falsely) that they cannot. What is harder to determine, of course, are the details of the ways in which such managerial impulses for discovering methods to improve the odds can be reconciled with standard, rational-calculation-based decisions to induce more sensible managerial risk taking.

Managers live and operate in a world characterized by uncertainty and by choice dilemmas, and, although acknowledging the calculus of risk taking, they find it often difficult to apply it in the real world, where actual outcomes count much more than elaborated calculations. This duality of calculation versus the eventual need to face the outcome of one's decision may tilt the pendulum to a search for ways to stand firm in the face of failure. This duality is nicely captured in Werfel's (1944) hilarious dialogue between Jacobowsky and Colonel Stjerbinsky in World War II Paris, where they were planning how to flee from the approaching enemy. In presenting his way of thinking (or rather espoused way of thinking), Jacobowsky said, "I, sir, believe in the laws of probability, for I am a lover of mathematics and logic. Why, I ask myself should I, among four million Parisians, fall victim to a bomb? The mathematical fraction of this probability is so infinitesimally small." He then went on to analyze the situation, uttering his famous phrase, "there are always two possibilities." In reacting to this logic, Colonel Stjerbinsky, invoking the societal role of an officer, responded by saying, "It's all the same! I do not know how many possibilities there are in life, two or five thousand. For a real man . . . for a real man . . . there is only one possibility."

Part 4

EPILOGUE

EPILOGUE

The managers who participated in this study differed on many dimensions in terms of their personal characteristics, their experience, and their domains of activity. However, they all shared one thing in common: They were all successful managers who held positions in organizations. Many experienced failure before they participated in the study and most likely experienced failure after that time. But at the time they took part in the study they were, by definition, successful, as attested to by their actual managerial positions.

It is possible that some of the findings were a reflection of the fact that these managers were successful. It seems plausible that successful managers might develop a heightened sense of personal control in decision making and risk taking. Possibly, many who failed might have some reservations about personal control. To examine such a possibility a sample of failed executives would be required. However, this is not a realistic strategy, since most executives can be considered failures at some point in time and successes at others. Getting a sample of executives at the time they are considered failures would be rather difficult. Furthermore, the sample in this study was quite diverse, and analysis of responses by industry and by sector did not reveal any significant differences. By and large, the differences were small. This is true also for the cross-cultural context of the study; indeed, the results were so similar that several statements made by the executives (such as "cutting corners" and "arranging for a blanket") could have literally been translated from English to Hebrew or vice versa.

Intrigued, however, by the potential effect of success on risk attitudes, I set out to re-interview two of the original 50 executives. Some of them had retired; some had moved to different corporations. I interviewed one manager, a former vice president of a high-tech firm in Silicon Valley, whose firm had gone under, and he was looking for another job or to start a new company. Needless to say, he is a rather wealthy person, so the failure of his company has caused him lots of grief but no personal financial problems. The other executive is the president of a high-tech corporation in Israel. This company is very successful, employs more than 100 people, and has recently gone public. Both of these executives were interviewed in 1985 and again in 1993. I went over the same protocol with them and recorded their responses.

The results of the interviews were very similar, both between the two of them and in comparison with their original responses in 1985. Both defined risk in 1993 as having to do with the downside part of the distribution, pertaining to the volume of investment. They disregarded probabilities as input to a decision problem. In the words of the Israeli manager, "people don't use probabilities in a reliable way, you can't count on that." Both said that survival was their major concern in risk taking, and the Israeli manager said that, although he had a larger safety net in 1993, he still considered the "worst-case scenario" in evaluating projects. He also set constraints on the amount to be invested and did not aggregate over projects. Rather, he considered every project separately.

Asked whether they believed in the correlation between risk and return, both responded in a negative manner. What advice would they give to a new or prospective manager? "Choose another, safer industry" said the California manager. "Start carefully but try to make some kind of a mark within a year," said the Israeli executive. He added that he thought the critical variable in his company's future was the quality of managers he could choose to work with him. He said that he selected these managers on the basis of his intuition; he used formal selection techniques only for choosing low-level managers.

Asked what they would say if they reflected on past decisions that turned out badly, the California manager said that, although he was well aware of several mistakes he had made in the past, he didn't think that, given the situation at the time, he would have decided otherwise. The Israeli manager acknowledged that he had made many mistakes, most of which he forgot about except those "missed opportunities," which he very well remembers. Both felt that they could achieve control over risky situations in their area of expertise. The sense of personal control did not diminish with the California executive; at most he was willing to attribute his company's demise to external economic forces beyond his control.

In responding to a question about what might be the major ingredient of sound managerial risk taking, they both said that it was intuition. Through years of experience, they said, intuition develops into the major tool (or decision aid) a manager can use in making risky choices.

Finally, I remembered that the younger children of these executives were either approaching college age or were in college. I recalled, from the first interview, their conservative attitudes regarding their children's education. I then asked them if they had considered alternatives regarding their children's college education. "Definitely not," responded the Californian, "You take no risks whatsoever with the education of your children." "Not at all," replied the Israeli manager, "I consider only the best, the business of your child's education is . . . too risky."

REFERENCES

Adams, D. (1975). "The decision making process utilized by U.S. Army field grade officers." *Military Review,* February, 14–25.

Adler, S. (1980). "Risk making management." *Business Horizons, 23,* 11–14.

Aggarwal, R., and C. Gibson. (1989). *Discounting in Financial Accounting and Reporting: Issues and Literature.* Morristown, NJ: Financial Executives Research Foundation.

Aharoni, Y. (1981). *The No Risk Society.* Chatham, NJ: Chatham House.

Alchian, A., and H. Demsetz. (1972). "Production information costs and economic organization." *American Economic Review, 62,* 777–795.

Alderfer, C. P., and H. Bierman, Jr. (1970). "Choices with risk: Beyond the mean and variance." *Journal of Business, 43,* 341–353.

Allais, M. (1953). "Le comportement de l'homme rationnel devant le risque: Critique des postulats et axiomes de l'école américaine." *Econometrica, 21,* 503–546.

Andrews, E. (1990). "The illogical process of invention." *New York Times,* May 5.

Arnold, J. (1986). "Assessing capital risk: You can't be too conservative." *Harvard Business Review, 64,* 113–121.

Arrow, K. J. (1965). *Aspects of the Theory of Risk Bearing.* Helsinki: Yrjo Jahnssonis Saatio.

Baker, G., M. Jensen, and K. Murphy. (1988). "Compensation and incentives: Practice vs. theory." *Journal of Finance, 43,* 593–616.

Bazerman, M. H. (1994). *Judgment in Managerial Decision Making.* New York: Wiley, 3rd Ed.

Beck, U. (1992). *Risk Society.* Newbury Park, CA: Sage.

Bell, D., H. Raiffa, and A. Tversky. (1988). "Descriptive, normative and prescriptive interactions in decision making." In D. Bell, H. Raiffa, and A. Tversky (Eds.), *Decision Making*. New York: Cambridge University Press.

Bernoulli, D. (1738). "Specimen theoriae novae de mensura sortis." *Commentarii Academiae Imperiales Petropolitanae, 5*, 175–192.

Boussard, J. M., and M. Petit. (1967). "Representation of farmers' behavior under uncertainty with focus-loss constraint." *Journal of Farm Economics, 49*, 869–880.

Bowman, E. H. (1980). "A risk-return paradox for strategic management." *Sloan Management Review, 21*, 17–31.

Bowman, E. H. (1982). "Risk seeking by troubled firms." *Sloan Management Review, 23*, 33–42.

Bowman, E., and H. Kunreuther. (1988). "Post-Bhopal behavior at a chemical company." *Journal of Management Studies, 25*, 387–402.

Brenner, M., and Z. Shapira. (1983). "Environmental uncertainty as determining merger activity." In Walter Goldberg (Ed.), *Mergers: Motives, Modes, Methods*. New Brunswick, NJ: W. G. Nichols.

Brinton, C. (1938). *Anatomy of Revolution*, New York: W. W. Norton.

Brockhaus, R. H., Sr. (1980). "Risk taking propensity of entrepreneurs." *Academy of Management Journal, 23*, 509–520.

Bromiley, P., and S. Curley. (1992). "Individual differences in risk taking," In F. Yates (Ed.), *Risk Taking Behavior*. New York: Wiley.

Brown, R. (1970). "Do managers find decision theory useful?" *Harvard Business Review*, May-June, 78–79.

Brown, R. (1992). "The state of the art of decision analysis: A personal perspective." *Interfaces, 22*, 5-14.

Budescu, D. V., and T. S. Wallsten. (1985). "Consistency in interpretation of probabilistic phrases." *Organizational Behavior and Human Decision Processes, 36*, 391–405.

Capen, E., R. Clapp, and W. Campbell. (1971). "Competitive bidding in high risk situations." *Journal of Petroleum Technology, 23*, 641–653.

Cohen, M. D., J. G. March, and J. P. Olsen. (1972). "A garbage can model of organizational choice." *Administrative Science Quarterly, 17*, 1–25.

Coombs, C. H. (1983). *Psychology and Mathematics*. Ann Arbor, MI: University of Michigan Press.

Coombs, C., R. Dawes, and A. Tversky. (1970). *Mathematical Psychology: An Elementary Introduction*. Englewood Cliffs, NJ: Prentice-Hall.

Coombs, C., and P. Lehner. (1981). "Evaluation of two alternative models for a theory of risk: I, Are moments of distributions useful in assessing risk?" *Journal of Experimental Psychology: Human Perception and Performance, 7,* 1110–1123.

Cyert, R. M., and J. G. March. (1963). *A Behavioral Theory of the Firm.* Englewood Cliffs, NJ: Prentice-Hall.

Davis, D. (1985). "New projects: Beware of false economics." *Harvard Business Review, 63,* 95–101.

Dearborn, C., and H. Simon. (1958). "Selective perception: A note on the departmental identification of executives." *Sociometry, 21,* 140–144.

Deci, E. L. (1975). *Intrinsic Motivation.* New York: Plenum.

Dickson, P., and J. Giglierano. (1986). "Missing the boat and sinking the boat: A conceptual model of entrepreneurial risk." *Journal of Marketing, 50,* 58–70.

Douglas, M. (1990). "Risk as a forensic resource." *Daedalus, 119,* 1–16.

Douglas, M., and A. Wildavsky. (1982). *Risk and Culture.* Berkeley, CA: University of California Press.

Dutton, J. (1986). "Understanding strategic agenda building and its implication for managing change." *Scandinavian Journal of Management Studies, 3,* 3–24.

Edwards, W. (1954). "The theory of decision making." *Psychological Bulletin, 51,* 380–417.

Einhorn, H. (1986). "Accepting errors to make less error." *Journal of Personality Assessment, 50,* 387–395.

Einhorn, H., and R. Hogarth. (1978). "Confidence in judgment: Persistence of the illusion of validity." *Psychological Review, 85,* 395–416.

Ellsberg, D. (1961). "Risk, ambiguity, and the Savage axioms." *Quarterly Journal of Economics, 75,* 643–699.

Ericsson, K., and H. Simon. (1980). "Verbal reports as data." *Psychological Review, 87,* 215–251.

Fama, E. (1991). "Efficient capital markets: II." *Journal of Finance, 96,* 1575–1617.

Fama, E., and K. French. (1993). "Risk factors in the return on stocks and bonds." *Journal of Financial Economics, 33,* 3–56.

Fiegenbaum, A. (1990). "Prospect theory and the risk-return association: An empirical examination of 85 industries." *Journal of Economic Behavior and Organizations, 14,* 187–204.

Fiegenbaum, A., and H. Thomas. (1986). "Dynamic and risk measurement perspectives on Bowman's risk-return paradox for strategic management: An empirical study." *Strategic Management Journal, 7,* 395–408.

Fischhoff, B. (1975). "Hindsight ≠ foresight: The effect of outcome knowledge on judgment under uncertainty." *Journal of Experimental Psychology: Human Perception and Performance, 1,* 288–299.

Fischhoff, B., and R. L. Beyth. (1975). "'I knew it would happen' —Remembered probabilities of once-future things." *Organizational Behavior and Human Performance, 3,* 552–564.

Fischhoff, B., S. Lichtenstein, P. Slovic, S. L. Derby, and R. Keeney. (1981). *Acceptable Risk.* New York: Cambridge University Press.

Fischhoff, B., S. R. Watson, and C. Hope. (1984). "Defining risk." *Policy Science, 17,* 123–139.

Fishburn, P. C. (1977). "Mean-risk analysis with risk associated with below-target returns." *American Economic Review, 67,* 116–126.

Fisher, I. (1906). *The Nature of Capital and Income.* New York: Macmillan.

French, K., and J. Poterba. (1991). "Investor diversification and international equity markets." *American Economic Review, 81,* 222–226.

Friedman, A., and Z. Shapira. (1988). "Beliefs about promotion decisions." Working paper, Hebrew University.

Friedman, M., and L. Savage. (1948). "The utility analysis of choices involving risk." *Journal of Political Economy, 56,* 279–304.

Gabriel, T. (1989). "Cliffhanger." *New York Times Magazine,* Dec. 31, 20.

Galai, D., and Z. Shapira, (1994). "Project selection: Effects of judgmental errors, managerial compensation and incentives." Working paper, New York University, Stern School of Business.

Garud, R., P. Nayyar, and Z. Shapira. (1993). "Technological oversights and foresights." Paper presented at the annual meeting of the Academy of Management, Atlanta.

Garud, R., and A. Van de Ven. (1992). "An empirical evaluation of the internal corporate venturing process." *Strategic Management Journal, 13,* 93–109.

Gibbons, M. R. (1982). "Multivariate tests of financial models: A new approach." *Journal of Financial Economics, 10,* 3–27.

Gilovich, T., R. Vallone, and A. Tversky. (1985). "The hot hand in basketball: On the misperception of random sequences." *Cognitive Psychology, 17,* 295–314.

Goleman, D. (1994). "Hidden rules often distort ideas of risk." *New York Times,* February 1.

Griffith, R. M. (1949). "Odds adjustments by American horse race bettors." *American Journal of Psychology, 62,* 290–294.

Hamilton, G. G. (1978). "The structural sources of adventurism: The case of the California gold rush." *American Journal of Sociology, 83,* 1466–1490.

Hastorf, A., and A. M. Isen. (Eds.). (1982). *Cognitive Social Psychology.* New York: Elsevier.

Heath, C., and A. Tversky. (1991). "Preferences and beliefs: Ambiguity and competence in choice under uncertainty." *Journal of Risk and Uncertainty, 4,* 5–28.

Heimer, C. (1988). "Social structure, psychology and the estimation of risk." *Annual Review of Sociology, 14,* 491–519.

Helson, H. (1964). *Adaptation Level Theory.* New York: Harper

Ibsen, H. (1884). *The Wild Duck.* Norton Critical Edition (1968), D. B. Cristiani (trans.). New York: W. W. Norton.

Jensen, M., and W. Meckling. (1976). "Theory of the firm: Managerial behavior, agency costs and ownership structure. *Journal of Financial Economics, 3,* 305–360.

Johnson, E. J., and A. Tversky. (1983). "Affect, generalization and the perception of risk." *Journal of Personality and Social Psychology, 45,* 20–31.

Kagel, J. (1989). "Judgmental errors in market settings: The winner's curse in the construction industry and OCS bidding." Working paper, University of Pittsburgh.

Kahneman, D. (1993). "Reference points, anchors, norms and mixed feelings." *Organizational Behavior and Human Decision Processes, 51,* 296–312.

Kahneman, D., R. Beyth-Marom, and Z. Lanir. (1984). "Probabilistic forecasting as decision-aid." Working paper, Hebrew University.

Kahneman, D., and D. Lovallo. (1993). "Timid choices and bold forecasts: A cognitive perspective on risk taking." *Management Science, 39,* 17–31.

Kahneman, D., and A. Tversky. (1979). "Prospect theory: An analysis of decision under risk." *Econometrica, 47,* 263–291.

Kahneman, D., and A. Tversky. (1982). "Variants of uncertainty." *Cognition, 11,* 143–157.

Kamil, A. C., and H. L. Roitblat. (1985). "The ecology of foraging behavior: Implications for animal learning memory." *Annual Review of Psychology, 36,* 141–169.

Kasperson, R., et al. (1988). "The social amplification of risk: A conceptual framework." *Risk Analysis, 8,* 177–187.

Kearns, D., and D. Nadler. (1992). *Prophets in the Dark: How Xerox*

Reinvented Itself and Beat Back the Japanese. New York: HarperCollins.

Keyes, R. (1985). *Chancing It.* Boston: Little, Brown.

Kingdon, J. (1984). *Agendas, Alternatives, and Public Policies.* Boston: Little, Brown.

Klamner, T. (1972). "Empirical evidence of the adoption of sophisticated capital budgeting techniques." *Journal of Business, 35*, 391–397.

Knight, F. (1921). *Risk, Uncertainty and Profit.* Boston: Houghton Mifflin.

Kogan, N., and M. A. Wallach. (1964). *Risk Taking.* New York: Holt, Rinehart & Winston.

Kuhl, J. (1978). "Standard setting and risk preference: An elaboration of the theory of achievement motivation and an empirical exploration." *Psychological Review, 85*, 239–248.

Kunreuther, H., et al. (1978). *Disaster Insurance.* New York: Wiley.

Kunreuther, H., R. Hogarth, and J. Meszaros. (1993). "Insurer ambiguity and market failure." *Journal of Risk and Uncertainty, 7*, 71–87.

Langer, E. J. (1975). "The illusion of control." *Journal of Personality and Social Psychology, 32*, 311–328.

Lanir, Z., and Z. Shapira. (1984). "Analysis of decisions concerning the defense of rear areas in Israel: A case study in defense decision making." In Z. Lanir (Ed.), *Israel's Security Planning in the 1980's.* New York: Praeger.

Lant, T. (1992). "Aspiration level adaptation: An empirical exploration." *Management Science, 38*, 623–644.

Laughhunn, D. J., J. W. Payne, and R. L. Crum. (1980). "Managerial risk preferences for below target returns." *Management Science, 26*, 1238–1249.

Lazear, E., and S. Rosen. (1981). "Rank order tournaments as optimum labor contracts." *Journal of Political Economy, 89*, 841–874.

Levinthal, D., and J. G. March. (1981). "A model of adaptive organizational search." *Journal of Economic Behavior and Organization, 2*, 307–333.

Levy, H., and H. M. Markowitz. (1979). "Approximating expected utility by a function of mean and variance." *American Economic Review, 69*, 308–317.

Levy, H., and M. Sarnat. (1984). *Portfolio and Investment Selection.* Englewood Cliffs, NJ: Prentice-Hall.

Lewin, K., T. Dembo, L. Festinger, and P. Sears. (1944). "Level of aspiration." In J. M. Hunt (Ed.), *Personality and the Behavior Disorders (Volume 1)*, 333–378. New York: Ronald Press.

Lindley, D. V. (1973). *Making Decisions.* London: Wiley.

Lopes, L. L. (1987). "Between hope and fear: The psychology of risk." *Advances in Experimental Social Psychology, 20,* 255–295.

Luce, R., and H. Raiffa. (1957). *Games and Decisions.* New York: Wiley.

McClelland, D. (1961). *The Achieving Society.* New York: D. Van Nostrand.

McInish, T. (1982). "Individual investors and risk-taking." *Journal of Economic Psychology, 2,* 125–136.

MacCrimmon, K. R., and D. A. Wehrung. (1986). *Taking Risks: The Management of Uncertainty.* New York: Free Press.

Mansfield, E. (1968). *The Economics of Technological Change.* New York: W. W. Norton.

Mao, J. (1970). "Survey of capital budgeting: Theory and practice." *Journal of Finance, 25,* 349–360.

March, J. G. (1978). "Bounded rationality, ambiguity, and the engineering of choice." *Bell Journal of Economics, 9,* 587–608.

March, J. G. (1981a). "Decisions in organizations and theories of choice." In A. Van de Ven and W. Joyce (Eds.), *Assessing Organizational Design and Performance.* New York: Wiley Interscience.

March, J. G. (1981b). "Footnotes to organizational change." *Administrative Science Quarterly, 26,* 563–577.

March, J. G. (1988a). "Variable risk preferences and adaptive aspirations." *Journal of Economic Behavior and Organization, 9,* 5–24.

March, J. G. (1988b). *Decisions and Organizations.* Oxford: Basil Blackwell.

March, J. G., and J. P. Olsen. (1976). *Ambiguity and Choice in Organizations.* Bergen, Norway: Universitetsforlaget.

March, J. G., and Z. Shapira. (1982). "Behavioral decision theory and organizational decision theory." In G. R. Ungson and D. N. Braunstein (Eds.), *Decision Making: An Interdisciplinary Inquiry,* 92–115. Boston: Kent.

March, J. G., and Z. Shapira. (1987). "Managerial perspectives on risk and risk taking." *Management Science, 33,* 1404–1418.

March, J. G., and Z. Shapira. (1992). "Variable risk preferences and the focus of attention." *Psychological Review, 99,* 172–183.

March, J. G., and H. A. Simon. (1958). *Organizations.* New York: Wiley.

Markoff, J. (1991). "And not a personal computer in sight." *New York Times,* October 6.

Markowitz, H. M. (1952). "The utility of wealth." *Journal of Political Economy, 60,* 151–158.

Markowitz, H. M. (1959). *Portfolio Selection.* New York: Wiley.

Mayhew, L. B. (1979). *Surviving the Eighties.* San Francisco: Jossey-Bass.

Maynard-Smith, J. (1978). "Optimization theory in evolution." *Annual Review of Ecology and Systematics, 9,* 31–56.

Menkus, B. (1988). "Don't rely too much on numbers." *Journal of Systems Management, 39,* 5.

Montgomery, H. (1989). "From cognition to action: The search for dominance in decision making." In H. Montgomery and O. Svenson (Eds.), *Process and Structure in Decision Making.* New York: Wiley.

Mueller, D. C. (1969). "A theory of conglomerate mergers." *Quarterly Journal of Economics, 83,* 643–659.

New York Times. (1992). "Brain cancer quickly disclosed." January 25.

Nichols, N. (1994). "Scientific management at Merck: An interview with CFO Judy Lewent." *Harvard Business Review, 72,* 89–99.

Nisbett, R., and T. Wilson. (1977). "Telling more than we can know: Verbal reports on mental processes." *Psychology Review, 84,* 231–259.

Norris, F. (1991). "If the numbers don't work, find new ones." *New York Times,* October 27, D1.

Noyce, R. (1978). "Innovation: The fruit of success." *Technology Review, 80,* 24–27.

Payne, J. (1973). "Alternative approaches to decision making under risk: Moments versus risk dimensions." *Psychological Bulletin, 80,* 439–453.

Payne, J. W., D. J. Laughhunn, and R. L. Crum. (1981). "Further tests of aspiration level effects in risky choice behavior." *Management Science, 27,* 953–958.

Peters, T., and R. Waterman. (1982). *In Search of Excellence.* New York: Harper & Row.

Petty, J., D. Scott, and M. Bird. (1975). "The capital expenditure decision making process of large corporations." *Engineering Economist, 20,* 159–172.

Porter, R. B. (1974). "Semi-variance." *American Economic Review, 64,* 200–204.

Pratt, J. W. (1964). "Risk aversion in the small and in the large." *Econometrica, 32,* 122–136.

Quiggin, S. (1982). "Theory of anticipated utility." *Journal of Economic Behavior and Organization, 3,* 323–343.

Raiffa, H. (1968). *Decision Analysis: Introductory Lectures on Choice under Uncertainty.* Reading, MA: Addison-Wesley.

Revelle, W., and E. Michaels. (1976). "The theory of achievement motivation revisited: The implications of inertial tendencies." *Psychological Review, 83,* 394–404.

Ross, S. A. (1981). "Some stronger measures of risk aversion in the small and in the large with applications." *Econometrica, 49,* 621–638.

Roy, A. (1952). "Safety first and the holding of assets." *Econometrica, 20,* 431–449.

Ruefli, T. (1990). "Mean-variance approaches to risk-return relationships in strategy: Paradox lost." *Management Science, 36,* 368–380.

Savage, L. (1954). *The Foundations of Statistics.* New York: Wiley.

Scherer, F. (1984). *Innovation and Growth.* Cambridge, MA: MIT Press.

Schoemaker, P. J. H. (1980). *Experiments on Decisions under Risk: The Expected Utility Hypothesis.* Boston: Martinus Nijhoff.

Schoemaker, P. J. H. (1982). "The expected utility model: Its variants, purposes, evidence and limitations." *Journal of Economic Literature, 20,* 529–563.

Shafir, E., I. Simonson, and A. Tversky. (1993). "Reason-based choice." *Cognition, 49,* 11–36.

Shapira, Z. (1975). "Measuring subjective probabilities by the magnitude production method." *Organizational Behavior and Human Performance, 14,* 314–321.

Shapira, Z. (1986). "Risk in managerial decision making." Unpublished manuscript, Hebrew University.

Shapira, Z. (1993). "Risk-sharing incentive contracts: On setting compensation policy for expatriate professionals in a foreign operation." In Y. Aharoni (Ed.), *Coalitions and Competition: The Globalization of Professional Business Services.* London: Routledge.

Shapira, Z., and I. Venezia. (1992). "Size and frequency of prizes as determinants of the demand for lotteries." *Organizational Behavior and Human Decision Processes, 52,* 307–318.

Sharpe, W. F. (1964). "Capital asset prices: A theory of market equilibrium under conditions of risk." *Journal of Finance, 19,* 425–442.

Sharpe, W. F. (1977). "The capital asset pricing model: A multi-beta interpretation." In H. Levy and M. Sarnat (Eds.), *Financial Decision Making under Uncertainty,* 127–136. New York: Academic Press.

Simon, H. A. (1947). *Administrative Behavior.* New York: Free Press.

Simon, H. A. (1955). "A behavioral model of rational choice." *Quarterly Journal of Economics, 69,* 99–118.

Singh, J. V. (1986). "Performance, slack and risk taking in strategic decisions." *Academy of Management Journal, 29,* 562–585.

Sitkin, S. B., and A. L. Pablo. (1992). "Reconceptualizing the determinants of risk behavior." *Academy of Management Review, 17,* 9–38.

Slovic, P. (1964). "Assessment of risk taking behavior." *Psychological Bulletin, 61,* 220–233.

Slovic, P. (1967). "The relative influence of probabilities and payoffs upon perceived risk of a gamble." *Psychonomic Science, 9,* 223–224.

Slovic, P. (1975). "Choice between equally valued alternatives." *Journal of Experimental Psychology: Human Perception and Performance, 1,* 280–287.

Slovic, P. (1987). "Perception of risk." *Science, 236,* 280–285.

Slovic, P., B. Fischhoff, and S. Lichtenstein. (1977). "Behavioral decision theory." *Annual Review of Psychology, 28,* 1–39.

Slovic, P., S. Lichtenstein, and B. Fischhoff (1982). "Facts versus fears: Understanding perceived risk." In D. Kahneman, P. Slovic and A. Tversky (Eds.), *Judgment under Uncertainty: Heuristics and Biases.* New York: Cambridge University Press.

Snyder, W. W. (1978). "Horse racing: Testing the efficient markets model." *Journal of Finance, 33,* 1109–1118.

Spencer, L. (1993). "When shunning risk costs lives." *Forbes,* December 20.

Sterner, J. (1990). *Other People's Money.* New York: Applause Theatre Publishing.

Strickland, L., R. J. Lewicki, and A. M. Katz. (1966). "Temporal orientation and perceived control as determinants of risk taking." *Journal of Experimental Social Psychology, 2,* 143–151.

Svenson, O. (1992). "Differentiation and consolidation theory of human decision making: A frame of reference for the study of pre and post decision processes." *Acta Psychologica, 80,* 143–168.

Thaler, R. (1988). *The Winner's Curse.* New York: Free Press.

Thaler, R. (1990). *Quasi-Rational Economics.* New York: Russell Sage Foundation.

Thaler, R. H., and E. J. Johnson. (1990). "Gambling with the house money and trying to break even: The effects of prior outcomes on risky choice." *Management Science, 36,* 643–660.

Tversky, A. (1972). "Elimination by aspects: A theory of choice." *Psychological Review, 79, 143*-151.

Tversky, A., and D. Kahneman. (1974). "Judgment under uncertainty: Heuristics and biases." *Science, 185,* 1124-1131.

Tversky, A., and D. Kahneman. (1981). "The framing of decisions and the psychology of choice." *Science, 211,* 453-458.

Tversky, A., and D. Kahneman. (1982). "Causal schemes in judgment under uncertainty." In D. Kahneman, P. Slovic, and A. Tversky (Eds.), *Judgment under Uncertainty: Heuristics and Biases,* 117-128. New York: Cambridge University Press.

U.S. Small Business Administration. (1991). *The State of Small Business: A Report to the President.* Washington, DC: U.S. Government Printing Office.

Vlek, C., and P. J. Stallen. (1980). "Rational and personal aspects of risk." *Acta Psychologica, 44,* 273-300.

Von Neumann, J., and O. Morgenstern. (1944). *Theory of Games and Economic Behavior.* Princeton, NJ: Princeton University Press.

Waggenar, W. (1972). "Generation of random sequences by human subjects: A critical survey of the literature." *Psychological Bulletin, 7,* 65-72.

Wall Street Journal. (1981a). "Don't be afraid to fail."

Wall Street Journal. (1981b). "To win a bidding war doesn't insure success of merged companies." September 1.

Wall Street Journal. (1989). "Gauging investment risk still is uncertain despite many methods." August 30.

Weber, E. (1994). "From subjective probabilities to decision weights: The effects of asymmetric loss functions on the evaluation of uncertain outcomes and events." *Psychological Bulletin, 115,* 228-242.

Weinstein, N. D. (1980). "Unrealistic optimism about future life events." *Journal of Personality and Social Psychology, 39,* 806-820.

Werfel, F. (1944). *Jacobowsky and the Colonel.* (G. Arlt, trans.). New York: Viking.

Wriston, W. (1986). *Risk and Other Four Letter Words.* New York: Harper & Row.

Yaari, M. (1987). "The dual theory of choice under risk." *Econometrica, 55,* 95-115.

Yates, F. (Ed.). (1992). *Risk Taking Behavior.* New York: Wiley.

Yates, F., and E. Stone. (1992). "The risk construct." In F. Yates (Ed.) *Risk Taking Behavior.* New York: Wiley.

Appendix 1

St. Petersburg Paradox:
Calculation of the expected utility of the gamble in Figure 1.2.

Following the proposal by the eighteenth century mathematician Cramer (cited in Bernoulli, 1738), the square root is used for the utility of outcomes. Thus,

$$U(x) = \sqrt{x}$$

Looking at the data in Table 1.1 we can, without loss of generality, divide the entries of the payoff column by 2. The expected value of the game is still infinity. Using the square root function, note that the expected utility of the game forms an infinitely decreasing sequence with a ratio smaller than 1. The expected utility can be calculated as follows:

$$EU(x) = \sum_{x=1}^{\infty} p(x)U(x) = \sum_{n=1}^{\infty} \frac{1}{2^n} \cdot \sqrt{2^{n-1}}$$

$$= \frac{1}{2} + \frac{\sqrt{2}}{4} + \frac{\sqrt{2} \cdot \sqrt{2}}{8} + \cdots \quad = \frac{1}{2} \cdot \frac{1}{1 - \frac{\sqrt{2}}{2}} = \frac{1}{2 - \sqrt{2}} = 1.707.$$

The maximal amount one should be willing to pay to participate in this gamble is therefore x_0,

where $\qquad\qquad\qquad EU(x) = U(x_0)$

and $\qquad\qquad\qquad x_0 = [EU(x)]^2.$

Therefore $\qquad\qquad x_0 = \left(\frac{1}{2-\sqrt{2}}\right)^2 = (1.707)^2 = \$2.914.$

The result is surprising, given that the gamble has an expected value of infinity.

Appendix 2

Survey questionnaire: Risk taking in managerial decision making.

The purpose of this questionnaire is to examine the role of risk taking in organizational decison making. Please feel free to raise any aspect or point of view that seems to be related to the subject. Your responses will be kept confidential.

A. Think of a decision you have recently made or were involved with in which there was an element of risk.

(1) Describe the decision.
(2) What are the risky elements in the decision?

_____

_____

_____

_____

_____

_____

_____

_____

_____

_____

B. Some people identify risk with uncertainty. What, in your opinion, is the relationship between risk and uncertainty?

_____

_____

_____

_____

_____

_____

B1. What do you think best describes the relation between risk and uncertainty? (Choose one, put an X next to it.)

_____   (1) Uncertainty leads to risk.

_____   (2) Uncertainty and risk are always related.

_____   (3) Uncertainty and risk are only sometimes related.

_____   (4) There is no relation between risk and uncertainty.

C1. Some people argue that concepts like gamble, chance, luck, game of chance, describe the notion of risk. Which of those concepts describe risk?

                    Concept (Y/N)   Reason

Gamble _____

Chance _____

Luck _____

Game _____

C2. Would you define risk taking in managerial decision making as gambling? If so, in what sense? Is risk taking similar to playing with dice? (Use numbers from the scale.)

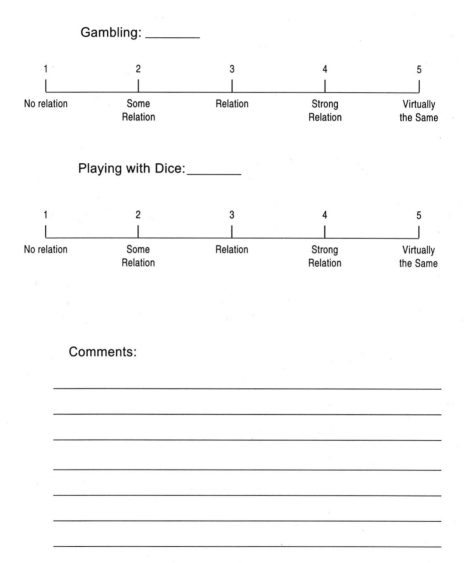

Gambling: _____

1	2	3	4	5
No relation	Some Relation	Relation	Strong Relation	Virtually the Same

Playing with Dice: _____

1	2	3	4	5
No relation	Some Relation	Relation	Strong Relation	Virtually the Same

Comments:

C3. Describe gambling and risk taking in managerial decision making by the degree to which you feel you have control in the situation. (Use a number from the scale.)

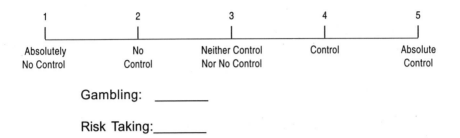

1	2	3	4	5
Absolutely No Control	No Control	Neither Control Nor No Control	Control	Absolute Control

Gambling: _____

Risk Taking:_____

C4. Describe the same two concepts by the degree to which you feel you can use your skills in dealing with such a situation. (Use numbers from the scale.)

1	2	3	4	5
Always Luck	Mainly Luck	Neither Skill Nor Luck	Mainly Use of Skills	Considerable Use of Skills

Gambling: _____

Risk Taking:_____

D. Rate the degree to which the following concepts characterize risk in managerial decision making. (Use numbers from the scale.)

1	2	3	4	5
Not at All	Does Not Characterize Risk	Not Sure	Does Characterize Risk	Very Clearly Characterizes Risk

—— 1. Information —— 2. Intuition —— 3. Control

—— 4. Survival of —— 5. Not achieving —— 6. Loss
      the firm   a goal

—— 7. Not achieving a time goal (deadline)

—— 8. Other (Explain)

_____

_____

_____

_____

_____

_____

_____

_____

E. It is usually thought that risk is related to return or profit, namely, when taking larger risks there is, on average, an expectation of a larger return. What is your opinion regarding this argument?

_____

_____

_____

_____

_____

_____

_____

E1. In your opinion (choose one, put an X next to it):

    ____ (1) Return is always related to risk.

    ____ (2) Return is conditionally dependent on risk.

    ____ (3) Return is not necessarily related to risk.

    ____ (4) There is no relation between risk and return.

E2. Please rate the relation of risk and return on the following scale:

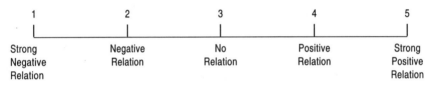

1	2	3	4	5
Strong Negative Relation	Negative Relation	No Relation	Positive Relation	Strong Positive Relation

Comments:

_____

_____

_____

_____

_____

_____

F. Another version of this relation suggests that "If you don't take risks there will be no returns." What is your opinion about this statement? (First, mark your response on the scale by circling a number and then explain.)

1	2	3	4	5
Not True	True Sometimes	True Beyond a Certain Level	True for Large Returns Only	Always True

Explain:

_____

_____

_____

_____

_____

_____

G. When you have to make a decision involving risk and you can buy insurance, in what conditions will you buy insurance and when will you assume the risk? (Possible examples: car insurance, health and life insurance, house insurance, insuring particular items.)

Fill in the table.

Domain	I'll buy insurance	Reason for buying insurance
	Always - 1 Often - 2 Sometimes - 3 Rarely - 4 Never - 5	Economic calculation - 1 Premium/loss ratio - 2 Peace of mind - 3 Other (specify) - 4
Health	_____	_____
Life	_____	_____
Assets	_____	_____
Other (specify)	_____	_____

H. What do you do when you are faced with a problem that involves risk? In particular, do you do any of the following? (Please rank 1, where it would be the most descriptive, through 7 the least descriptive.)

	Rank Order
a. Avoid taking risks	_____
b. Collect more information	_____
c. Check different aspects of the problem	_____
d. Actively work on the problem to reduce the risk	_____
e. Delay the decision	_____
f. Delegate the decision	_____
g. Other (specify)	_____

I. Are there any conditions or situations where organizations should:

(1) take risks?
(2) avoid taking risks?

What are the critical determinants of taking risks in this regard?

(1) Take risks:

_____

_____

_____

_____

_____

(2) Avoid taking risks:

_____

_____

_____

_____

J. Observing other managers who are your superiors, peers or subordinates, can you identify risk-prone versus risk-averse managers?
How?

   a. Risk-Prone:

_____
_____
_____
_____
_____

   b. Risk-Averse:

_____
_____
_____
_____
_____

J1. If a new manager would ask your advice regarding risk taking, what advice would you give him/her? In particular, would you advise the new manager to (rank, 1 = most probable advice; 4 = least probable):

_____ (a) Avoid taking risks.

_____ (b) Take a variety of precautionary measures if he/she has to take risks.

_____ (c) Learn the situation, reduce the risk, and take only calculated risks.

_____ (d) Do take risks.

Please explain the main consideration in this advice:

_____

_____

_____

_____

_____

K. Are there any arrangements in your organization regarding risk taking? Are there incentives and penalties involved with risk taking? Are you pleased with these arrangements? Why?

Arrangements:

_____

_____

_____

Incentives:

_____

_____

_____

Penalties:

_____

_____

_____

L. Do you conceive of risk in terms of the probability distribution of (rank, 1 = most descriptive; 3 = least descriptive):

_____ (a) the entire possible outcomes.

_____ (b) the positive outcomes only.

_____ (c) the negative outcomes only.

M. Do you usually accept risk estimates provided to you by other people as a given or do you try to (rank, 1 = most descriptive; 4 = least descriptive):

_____ (a) check them.

_____ (b) modify the parameters of risk.

_____ (c) work on the estimates so that risk becomes acceptable.

_____ (d) other. (Specify.)

_____

_____

_____

N. There are people who distinguish among financial risk, technological risk, marketing risk, etc. Assuming all these dimensions exist, is it possible to express them in one number which characterizes the entire overall risk?

_____

_____

_____

_____

_____

_____

_____

O. Are there differences between risk taking in organizations and in personal life as in family financial affairs?

_____

_____

_____

_____

_____

_____

_____

_____

P. Consider yourself in each of the following situations separately:

   a. You succeed a lot and are well above the target.

   b. You succeeded and are above the target.

   c. You barely succeeded and are hardly above the target.

   d. You failed a little and are hardly below the target.

   e. You failed and are below the target.

   f. You experienced considerable failure and are well below the target.

   For each situation, separately indicate 3 numbers describing the risk that:

   You would take

   You should have taken

   Other managers would take

Numbers come from the following scale:

1 = Minimum risk
2 = Definitely less than average risk
3 = A little less than average risk
4 = Average risk
5 = A little more than average risk
6 = Definitely more than average risk
7 = Maximum risk

Please fill those numbers in on the table.

Risk Situation	a	b	c	d	e	f
I would have taken						
I should have taken						
Other managers would take						

Q. Think about previous risky decisions that you have taken—some that have succeeded as well as those that were not successful. Reflecting on these, do you think that risk can be managed? In what ways?

_____

_____

_____

_____

_____

_____

_____

R. An executive said recently "logically and personally, I am willing to take more risk (in percentages) the more assets I have." Could you please comment on this statement?

_____

_____

_____

_____

_____

S. Suppose your company is in a terrible situation and close to bankruptcy. You still have a sizable amount of money that you kept for such a disaster. For various reasons you have only two options in using it. One option involves an investment in a risky project that has a 55% chance of doubling your money and a 45% chance of losing it all. The alternative is a nonrisky option that will give you 10% return in about the same time. Which option would you choose? Why?

_____

_____

_____

_____

_____

_____

_____

_____

_____

_____

Background data:

Name of organization: _____

Job Title: _____

Level in Organization: ____   1. Highest level management
                       ____   2. Senior level management
                       ____   3. Medium level management
                       ____   4. Lower level management

Type of Organization: Small _____   Private Sector _____

                         Medium _____   Public Sector _____

                         Large _____

Age: _____

Sex: Female _____   Male _____

Date of Filling in Questionnaire: _____

Thank You!

INDEX

Boldface numbers refer to figures and tables.

Brown, R., 129, 139
Budescu, D. V., 23, 139

Campbell, W., 79, 139
Capen, E., 79, 139
capital asset pricing model, 23
capital budgeting, 95
causal basis of events, 27
certainty, 4, 11
chance, 46, 48, 126
Chief Executive Officers (CEOs), 127
children, 137
choice, 4–5, 9–10, 94, 104; argument-based, 103; behavioral model of rational, 12. *See also* risky choice; timid choices
Clapp, R., 79, 139
cliff-hanging, 81
Cochlear Implants project, 115
coded responses, 39, 41
cognitive perspectives, 120–121
Cohen, M. D., 97, 139
coin, flipping a fair, 4, 5–8, 19, 93
comparisons: cross-respondent, 35; for managerial thinking, 69; of normative and descriptive perspectives, 14–16
compensation, executive, 127
competition, 115, 116
confidence, 81–82
conflict, 103
construction business, 78–79
context, 31, 66, 68, 70–71
contractors, 79
contracts, 79, 121–123
control, 27, 74, 125, 128, 132; belief in postdecisional, 78–80, 81, 104; in laboratory situations, 33; over performance targets, 115–117; in risk taking, 46, 48, **48**, 49, 52, 81, 82
Coombs, C. H., 20, 23, 89, 139, 140
corporations, 129; state-owned, **50**, **77**. *See also* organizations
costs, 108; responsibility, 124–125
Creasey, J., 130

Crum, R. L., 25, 34, 143, 145
Curley, S., 73, 139
Cyert, R. M., 12, 72, 96, 97, 140

Davis, D., 131, 140
Dawes, R., 20, 139
dealing with risks, 22, 26–28, 38, 72; findings on, 41, 82; modes of, 75–78, **76, 77**
Dearborn, C., 122, 140
Deci, E. L., 25, 54, 140
decision criterion: lowering the, **112**; raising the, **111**; shifts of, 110–112
decision makers, 96, 127; attitudes toward risk of, 22, 23–24, 26–27; below performance target, 97; traits of risk-averse and risk-seeking, 26
decision making, 78, 132; errors in, 108; improving risk taking in managerial, 125; investment, 107, 108; in laboratory settings, 34; managerial, 49, 80, 104, 116; in organizations, 32, 56, 129; personal, 125; in realistic situations involving risky choices, 21–22; risk taking in managerial, 48, **48**; risk taking and responsibility in organizational, 121–122, 123, 125; role of risk in, 3–5; rules affecting, 98; teaching, xii; under uncertainty, 106–107
decision-making situations: principles for, 11–12; types of, 4
decision rules, 98, 100
decisions, 106, 136–137; business, 39, 40; investment, 110; managerial, 38, 78, 80, 107, 122–123, 126; multiple, 118; personal, 39, 40; ramifications of, 116; relation between future outcomes and, **109**, 117; risk attitudes and the context of, 60; risky, 123; types of, 39–40. *See also* targets